GOTTFRIED SEMPER
(1803–1879)

OTTO WAGNER
(1841–1918)

DANIEL BURNHAM
(1846–1912)

ANTONI GAUDÍ
(1852–1926)

LOUIS SULLIVAN
(1856–1924)

VICTOR HORTA
(1861–1947)

FRANK LLOYD WRIGHT
(1867–1959)

AUGUSTE PERRET
(1874–1954)

WALTER GROPIUS
(1883–1969)

LUDWIG MIES VAN DER ROHE
(1886–1969)

LE CORBUSIER
(1887–1965)

GERRIT RIETVELD
(1888–1987)

RICHARD NEUTRA
(1892–1970)

ALVAR AALTO
(1898–1976)

CLAUDE-NICOLAS LEDOUX
(1736–1806)

THOMAS JEFFERSON
(1743–1826)

KARL FRIEDRICH SCHINKEL
(1781–1841)

LOUIS I. KAHN
(1901–1974)

PHILIP JOHNSON
(1906–2005)

OSCAR NIEMEYER
(1907–2012)

EERO SAARINEN
(1910–1961)

KENZŌ TANGE
(1913–2005)

IEOH MING PEI
(*1917)

GÜNTER BEHNISCH
(1922–2010)

CESAR PELLI
(*1926)

FRANK O. GEHRY
(*1929)

ALDO ROSSI
(1931–1997)

RICHARD ROGERS
(*1933)

RICHARD MEIER
(*1934)

NORMAN FOSTER
(*1935)

GERKAN, MARG
UND PARTNER
(*1935 & 1936)

SOM
(GEGRÜNDET: 1936)

RAFAEL MONEO
(*1937)

RENZO PIANO
(*1937)

TADAO ANDŌ
(*1941)

TOYO ITO
(*1941)

REM KOOLHAAS
(*1944)

JEAN NOUVEL
(*1945)

DANIEL LIBESKIND
(*1946)

STEVEN HOLL
(*1947)

ZAHA HADID
(1950–2016)

HERZOG & DE MEURON
(*1950 & *1950)

1700   1800   1900   1935

50 ARCHITECTS

YOU SHOULD KNOW

Isabel Kuhl
Kristina Lowis
Sabine Thiel-Siling

PRESTEL

Munich · London · New York

CONTENTS

FILIPPO BRUNELLESCHI

A skilled goldsmith as well as a painter and sculptor, Brunelleschi became one of the great architects of the early Renaissance. He was inundated commissions in the wealthy city-state of Florence, as influential families and guilds built an abundance architectural works in their own honor.

FILIPPO BRUNELLESCHI

1377 Born in Florence, Italy

1401 Takes part in the competition for the design of the Baptistery Doors in Florence, which is won by Lorenzo Ghiberti

1404 Becomes a member of the guild of Florentine goldsmiths

1418 Submits plans for the competition for the design of the Florence cathedral dome

1420 Begins work on the cathedral dome

1420s The Old Sacristy in San Lorenzo, Florence

1430 Begins work on the Pazzi Chapel, Santa Croce, Florence

1436 Receives the contract to build the the cathedral's dome lantern

1446 Dies April 16, in Florence

In about 1419, Brunelleschi, the son of a notary, was pleased to receive two important commissions at once. The guild of silk makers commissioned him to build a house for the foundlings of Florence. In creating the Ospedale degli Innocenti, he returned to classical elements of building, always intent on symmetry of design and harmonious proportions, from façades to interior rooms. The second commission that year came from the very highest of circles. A member of the influential Medici family, Giovanni d'Averardo, ordered a chapel for his tomb from Brunelleschi. He designed the Old Sacristy (as it was later called, to distinguish it from Michelangelo's New Sacristy) in the Florentine church of San Lorenzo as a central-plan building. On a square ground plan, a hemisphere arches over the space—the decisive forms are the cube and square. The client was so enthusiastic about Brunelleschi's design for the Old Sacristy that he immediately entrusted to him the rebuilding of the entire church.

But not all Florentines expected great things of Brunelleschi. The wool workers' guild, for example, which was responsible for building the cathedral, seemed rather hesitant. It was a question of crowning the cathedral, the flagship of the city, with a dome. The diameter of the octagonal substructure already stood at a proud 45 meters. There was no question—for such a task, a first-class master architect had to be engaged. Several applicants believed themselves capable of it and took part in a competition. The judges were undecided. It was only after two years that they were convinced by Brunelleschi's proposal. The new project manager was not afraid of innovations: he clothed the dome in two shells, of which only the inner one is load-bearing, so that he could reduce the overall weight of the dome. Brunelleschi was also inventive with regard to the organization of the work; in order to spare the workers in the dome the tedious and time-consuming climb up and down at midday, he had wine taverns and kitchens built under the church roof.

But the clients were skeptical about Brunelleschi's inventiveness. In 1432, when it was a question of the design of the crowning lantern of the dome, the guild preferred to hold a further competition, rather than leave this task to Brunelleschi. In the end it was his design that was executed, but he did not live to see the completion of the dome: he died in 1446. Giorgio Vasari reported on the funeral of the great architect in Florence cathedral, without concealing that his native land "honored him far more greatly after his death than it had done during his lifetime."

Cathedral of Santa Maria del Fiore (dome), Florence, 1420–1436

LEON BATTISTA ALBERTI

Archaeologist and painter, musician and scientist—to call Leon Battista Alberti multi-talented would be an understatement. Particularly since Alberti also found time to dedicate himself to architecture, and thus definitively secure his reputation as a Renaissance "universal man."

Alberti approached architecture in a roundabout way. At first he made an intensive study of the buildings of classical antiquity, above all as they were still to be admired in Rome, and at the same time read with enthusiasm the writings of classical architects. Spurred on by their works, Alberti also wrote a treatise on architectural theory, *De re aedificatoria*. But his knowledge of classical buildings was reflected not only on paper: the palaces and churches designed by him also clearly mirror this deep admiration.

Alberti's first large commission came from the Rucellai, a wealthy Florentine family of merchants; he was to design their spacious residence on the central Via della Vigna. Alberti drew up the plans and the Rossellino workshop carried out the execution. The façade of the palace alone showed the architect to be a fan of the classical style: he adorned the house with an order of columns similar to those of the Colosseum in Rome. But in doing this he did not use rounded columns, but flat wall columns know as pilasters for the vertical emphasis. At the same time, he stressed the horizontal lines by placing cornices between the stories. In this way, the façade of the mansion appears clearly structured, and the impression of symmetry and fine proportions is achieved.

It was not only Giovanni Rucellai who had confidence in Alberti's talents. Not far from his city mansion, the Dominican church of Santa Maria Novella was awaiting completion. The Gothic structure was already nearly finished, and even the foundation of the façade had already been begun when the clients commissioned Alberti to complete it. He therefore had to incorporate his knowledge of classical temple architecture into the existing fabric. Thus Gothic pointed arches stand under niches and portals in the lower zone, and above them are superimposed round arches. Sweeping volutes lead from the broad substructure to the sharp gable, forms from the Gothic and Renaissance styles combine harmoniously, and everything glows in white and green stone.

It was on Alberti, who remained unmarried all his life, that the choice of the ruler of Rimini fell when he planned to erect a memorial to his wife. Sigismondo Pandolfo Malatesta commissioned a tomb for himself and his family, conceived, in disregard of Christian traditions, as a pagan temple. He himself and his Isotta were to be buried there, and instead of symbols of the cross, it was decorated with the entwined letters *S* and *I* in abundance. Alberti admittedly did not concern himself with the adornment of the interior, but once again designed the façade. In the Tempio Malatestiano, too, the architect did not conceal his preference for classical forms: the central part of the frontage, for example, goes back to the closely related triumphal arch of the Roman Emperor Augustus.

Santa Maria Novella, Florence, façade 1456–1470

03

DONATO BRAMANTE

Bramante's father had decided that his son should be a painter. Donato submitted, but met with a distinct lack of success, as noted by Gorgio Vasari: "So he determined, in order to view an important building at least once, to go to Milan and look at the cathedral."

DONATO BRAMANTE

ca. 1444
    Born near Urbino in today's Fermignano, Italy

1476 Moves to Milan

ca. 1480
    Extension to Santa Maria presso Santo Satiro, Milan, begun

1499 Moves to Rome

1500–04
    Cloistered courtyard of Santa Maria della Pace, Rome

1502 Monastery of San Pietro in Montorio, Tempietto, Rome

1503 Pope Julius II commissions him to build St. Peter's Basilica

1514 Dies April 11, in Rome

Bramante's visit to Milan was momentous, for the young painter decided on the spot to become an architect. He began by making an intensive study of the classical buildings of Rome. His first commissions brought him back to Milan, but finally, after all, he settled in the capital. In the early 16th century Rome was a great and prestigious place to build, and above all it was the popes who brought many notable architects to the city.

It was on the Gianicolo, a hill on the right bank of the Tiber, that Donato Bramante worked on his first architectural commission. The monastery of San Pietro in Montorio was to be enriched by a memorial building to recall the martyrdom of the Apostle Peter, which was said to have taken place there. Bramante decided in favor of a central-plan structure on a circular base—that the surrounding monastery courtyard would eventually be rectangular was something the architect could not have foreseen. Three steps, arranged in circles around the structure, lead up to the small temple, the *Tempietto*. Columns surround the circular building, crowned with a dome, and there is a balustrade on the upper level. Bramante's Tempietto was regarded by the next generation as a perfect central-plan building, an architectural type that was considered the epitome of ideal beauty.

The Renaissance embodiment of the mania for building was undoubtedly Pope Julius II. Soon after his election in 1503 he took in hand the rebuilding of St. Peter's Basilica—the old building could neither accommodate the throngs of pilgrims nor satisfy the pope's ambitious demands. Julius had big plans and Bramante was part of them: he was to build a church that would do justice to the importance of Rome as the heart of Christendom. By 1506 Bramante's plans had progressed so far that the foundation stone could be laid. Bramante designed St. Peter's on the ground plan of a Greek cross, with four arms of equal length—another central-plan building, again crowned with a mighty dome.

With the basilica of St. Peter, Bramante had taken on the most important project in Rome, but the pope was no ordinary client: "To be honest," Bramante once summed it up, "they give you water and words, smoke and hot air. If you ask for more, you are dismissed." His fee was a comparatively small expense; the outrageous costs of the new building, despite the lively and controversial trade in indulgences, could not be covered. When Bramante died in 1514, only the choir area had made any progress, and subsequent generations of architects largely overruled his design—today's basilica reflects Bramante's plans at most in its gigantic proportions.

Tempietto, Rome, 1502–1505

MICHELANGELO

By his mid-30s, Michelangelo was already used to illustrious clients lining up to secure his services for their projects. So it seems only logical that at the advanced age of 71 he was personally requested by the pope to take over the most important building project of the era, the completion of St. Peter's Basilica in Rome.

MICHELANGELO

Michelangelo was already widely regarded as the greatest sculptor and painter of his day when he turned to architecture. The friend of his youth, Giovanni de' Medici, now Pope Leo X, had great plans for the family buildings in his home city of Florence. From 1516, Michelangelo gave expression to these wishes. For the church of San Lorenzo he designed a façade without parallel: twelve monumental columns, each one several tons in weight, were to adorn the marble frontage. However, only one of these survived unbroken from the quarry on the building site, and the many failures caused the building costs to soar. Michelangelo became enraged, the pope cancelled the contract, and promptly signed up the architect for another project. It was not the façade but a family vault that Michelangelo was now to tackle in San Lorenzo: between 1520 and 1534, the New Sacristy took shape (as a counterpart to Brunelleschi's Old Sacristy). The next commission followed immediately with the next Medici Pope: Clement VII had Michelangelo plan and execute the library of the monastery of San Lorenzo. The Biblioteca Medicea Laurenziana, designed in close cooperation with the pope, became Michelangelo's most important architectural work: the most prestigious one was still to come.

Equally at home with all genres of art, Michelangelo was now known as simply the universal genius. It was only to him that Pope Paul III would entrust the task of bringing the work on St. Peter's, which had been dragging along for decades, to a successful conclusion. Giorgio Vasari, friend and biographer of Michelangelo, noted the latter's enthusiastic reaction to the enquiry from Rome: "At last His Holiness decided, as I believe, by divine inspiration, to send for Michelangelo. Michelangelo tried to avoid the burden, saying that architecture was not his real field, and since his requests were of no avail, the Pope in the end positively ordered him to accept the commission." Admittedly, Paul III sweetened the deal for his chosen candidate, appointing the Florentine as chief director of building in 1547 and granting him powers that no other architect was ever to be given by a client: Michelangelo alone was to decide what should be torn down and what should be added. So much freedom summoned envious rivals who were not sparing in their criticisms. One reproach was that Michelangelo was designing only a small church of St. Peter, a "San Pietrino," instead of the greatest church in Christendom. Undeterred, Michelangelo reduced the size of his predecessor's model, certain that the effect of the central-plan building would only be increased as a result.

The chief architect of St. Peter's was already 71 when he took over the building project, and to provide against further changes to his plans by potential successors he ordered work to begin simultaneously on all the important areas of the building. It was a strategy that largely worked.

St. Peter's Basilica, Rome, Architect 1547–1564 (planning and construction)

Biblioteca Medicea Laurenziana, Florence, 1523–1560

New Sacristy in San Lorenzo, Florence, 1520–1524

05

ANDREA PALLADIO

Palladio's career reads like a rags-to-riches story: a miller's son from Padua, he went on to become one of the most sought-after architects of the wealthy. More than 60 villas, churches, and city mansions were built to his designs.

The skilled stonemason Andrea di Pietro was in his mid-20s when the writer and aristocrat Gian Giorgio Trissino recognized his talent. He bestowed the name Palladio on his protégé and traveled with him to Rome—a momentous trip for the young man. Back in the Veneto, over the next four decades Palladio followed classical principles of building—mainly for very wealthy clients, for Trissino opened many doors in high society to the young man in his lateral career move. In the 16th century, few prosperous families were without their own country villa, and their preferred architect was Andrea Palladio. His client Paolo Almerico commissioned from him a villa on a hill on the outskirts of Vicenza. A circular hall surmounted by a cupola forms the center of the building and gave it its name: the "Rotonda" is presented as a central-plan building—a daring design, for this ground plan was more usual in ecclesiastical buildings than in private houses. In the design the Rotunda's entrance, Palladio oriented himself to the temple frontages of classical antiquity, and gave the Rotonda no fewer than four of these. The comfort of the residents was not forgotten by the architect: he placed the utility rooms in the basement, while the piano nobile was reserved for celebrations, and the family lived in the mezzanine floor above.

When Palladio finally succeeded in establishing himself in Venice, many of his villas already adorned the mainland, the Veneto. In his mid-50s, he could at last make his mark in Venice, and with the location, the building tasks also changed: the Benedictine monks of the monastery on the island of San Giorgio commissioned an impressive three-aisled church with a dome, whose splendid façade (admittedly probably altered by a successor) faces towards the city. On the neighboring island of the Giudecca, Palladio, then almost 70 years old, also created an imposing house of God for the Capuchins. "Il Redentore," the church of the Redeemer, came into being as a memorial to mark the end of a plague epidemic, and this building too is adorned by a tiered, brilliantly white temple frontage. Palladio could no longer complain of a lack of variety.

His final commission too was a challenge: he was to build a theater *all'antica* (in the antique style) for the scholars of Vicenza. Once again he needed to satisfy cultured tastes, and once again he fell back on his studies of classical buildings and architectural treatises. With the help of ingenious perspective, the architect of villas was now in addition creating the theater of the Renaissance.

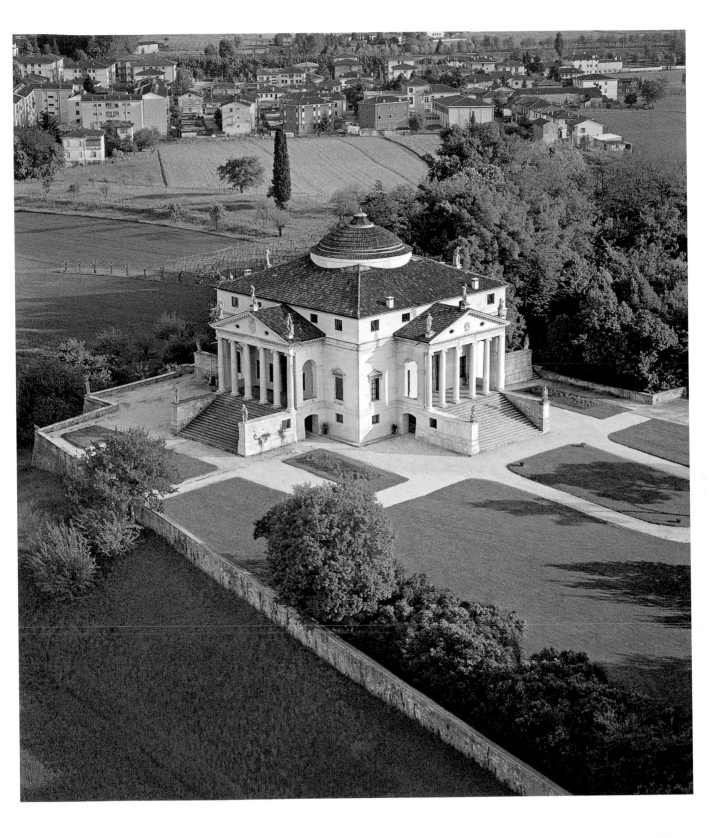

Rotunda, near Vincenza, 1566–1591

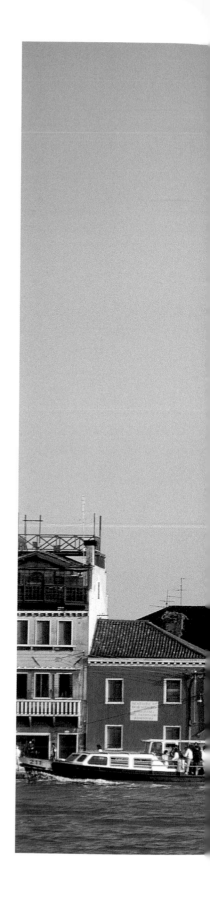

Il Redentore, Venice, 1575–1592

06

GIAN LORENZO BERNINI

As a seven-year-old, Gian Lorenzo Bernini, born in Naples, accompanied his sculptor father to Rome. Bernini first attracted attention as a sculptor, but soon he was in demand as an architect and it can be said that no other artist has had such a profound influence on Rome's cityscape.

GIAN LORENZO BERNINI

At the start of the 17th century, hardly a stone was still in its place in the Eternal City: streets and squares were laid out, and the Vatican was architecturally integrated into the city, for it was the popes themselves who were strenuously promoting urban modernization. And in the course of his career over more than six decades, Bernini was able to rely on the patronage of several popes. If he fell out of favor with the Vatican, there were still illustrious secular patrons to be found to make use of Bernini's services, including King Louis XIV of France. No wonder that Bernini did not hide his light under a bushel. When there was criticism of the nose in a newly completed portrait of Louis, he responded curtly: "That is how I see it."

Bernini combined his talents as a sculptor and architect in his largest and most spectacular fountain. In the middle of the Piazza Navona in Rome, four marble river gods are enthroned on a rock, representing the parts of the earth known at that time: the Ganges and the Nile, the Danube and the Rio de la Plata form the basis of the monumental Fountain of Four Rivers, from whose center a Roman obelisk towers up. In 1656, on the opposite bank of the Tiber, and within the Vatican City, Bernini began his most important project, the redesign of St. Peter's Square. From the viewpoint of the existing square, the effect of the mighty dome of the basilica was hardly to be perceived. Bernini first designed a trapezoid arrangement, and then toyed with the idea of a circular shape. Finally, he decided in favor of two adjoining areas, appropriate to the huge dimensions of the church: the Piazza Obliqua, 140 meters in depth, consists of an ellipse running diagonally to the church, to which is adjoined the Piazza Retta, which widens in trapezoid shape to 90 meters towards the basilica of St. Peter. At the edges of both areas, Bernini placed wide rows of columns to enclose the Baroque complex effectively.

A tireless worker, Bernini continually pursued parallel tasks to this one, including the building of the church of Sant'Andrea on the Quirinal Hill. The decisive shape of this Jesuit church is the oval, and the ground-plan oval is even set diagonally. A circular staircase leads up to the portal, which in its turn is shielded by a canopy. Curved walls project on to the street from the portal. Bernini's urge to design did not stop at the façade: the design extends to the interior too, where the oval forms are continued. The architect himself often visited the little church even after its completion, considering it one of his masterpieces.

Sant'Andrea al Quirinale, Rome, 1658–1670

St. Peter's Square, Rome, 1656– 1667

07

CHRISTOPHER WREN

Christopher Wren's name is synonymous with London's largest church, St. Paul's Cathedral, which kept its builder occupied for 35 years. At the age of 78, Wren had the great good fortune to see the completion of the building.

CHRISTOPHER WREN

At an early age, Christopher Wren, who grew up in a rural area of Wiltshire in the southwest of England, became enthusiastic about the sciences. After studying at Oxford, he began a professorship in London, and taught astronomy there and later in Oxford. That he was entrusted with building or restoring almost 50 churches, Wren owed not only to his talent, but also to a tragic accident. In September 1666, the Great Fire of London raged for four days and four nights. After the devastating fire, a huge program of rebuilding was speedily undertaken: 13,200 houses and 87 parish churches needed to be replaced. At this point in time, Wren had already become known with his first designs and buildings, and this was his opportunity to make his mark in the capital on a grand scale. Two years after the Great Fire, the self-taught architect was asked to draft a plan for the reconstruction of St. Paul's Cathedral, for this church dedicated to the Apostle Paul had also fallen victim to the fire. Wren suggested a central-plan building, such as was known in the Italian High Renaissance, but the clients rejected the proposal as being too daring (too Catholic) for a major Protestant church. Patience was the watchword over the years that followed, and it was not until 1675 that Wren's design, meanwhile greatly modified, found acceptance.

In the meantime Wren had finally decided in favor of architecture and against his post of professor of astronomy. His courage was rewarded by a plethora of commissions; in 1677 almost 30 of his designs were being executed at the same time. For St. Paul's, Wren relied on two quite different traditions, as he was able to draw on Renaissance architecture as much as on Baroque. The façade with two towers and a vestibule, supported by columns and crowned by a pediment, is reminiscent of classical temple frontages as Palladio had invoked them. In the interior, the space, arranged on a cruciform ground plan, opens upwards into a high cupola— Wren's trademark and, for a long time, a symbol of London.

Despite all the virtuality that the master builder dedicated to his grand project, other commissions received due attention. Wren remained attached to Oxford, where he had studied and later taught, as can be seen in the Sheldonian Theater, St. John's College, and Christ Church Tower. In Cambridge he designed, among other buildings, the library of Trinity College, and when he died in London at the venerable age of 91 he could also number among his buildings several palaces and hospitals he had built to royal commissions.

St. Paul's Cathedral, London, 1675–1709

08

JOHANN BALTHASAR NEUMANN

Whether it was a question of a new church or a magnificent palace, during the first half of the 18th century many important German clients favored only one man—the Bohemian-born Balthasar Neumann.

JOHANN BALTHASAR NEUMANN

Neumann's beginnings were comparatively modest. The son of two cloth-makers, he was apprenticed to his godfather, a metal caster. But as a 25 year old, having meanwhile moved to Würzburg, Neumann became deeply involved in other interests. He entered the artillery, which enabled him to begin a career as an engineer, and to receive further training in hydraulics, geometry, fortifications, and architecture.

Neumann's talents were in demand as early as 1715, when the influential Schönborn family commissioned him to build a fountain for the family palace. They were clearly satisfied with the result, for further commissions followed immediately. The Schönborns were to become the master builder's most important patrons. When Johann Philipp Franz von Schönborn was chosen as Prince-Bishop of Würzburg in 1719, his preferred architect was already in place: under Neumann's direction, work began on the Prince-Bishop's new residence. Together with Lucas von Hildebrandt, Maximilian von Welsch, and a number of other artists he created, over the next decade and a half, a superb complex, whose four wings surround a cour d'honneur (a courtyard for ceremonial occasions). For one of the structural high points, the impressive staircase, Neumann made himself personally responsible. From the entrance hall on the ground floor, a wide step leads to a gallery placed around the staircase. To ascend, visitors must first climb the lower flight of steps and thus reach a landing. Now they have to change direction and decide in favor of one of the two flights of stairs leading to the gallery. With this sophisticated arrangement, Neumann succeeded in directing the visitor's gaze slowly but surely upwards—above the white stucco decorations of the gallery walls, step by step there opens up a view of a monumental ceiling fresco, executed by the Venetian artist Giovanni Battista Tiepolo.

It was not only for innovative staircase designs that Neumann was engaged over the years that followed. He also found ample opportunities to prove himself in church architecture. He created a number of churches that clearly illustrate that there were no limits to his wealth of invention. In Vierzehnheiligen, a Bavarian pilgrimage church, for example, he created a ground plan composed of ovals of various sizes. The façade of the building, flanked by two towers, projects in the central area, and in the interior too Neumann stressed its three-dimensionality, so that the church appears almost to move—a feast for the eyes for both religious and architectural pilgrims.

Würzburger Residence, Würzburg, 1719–1741

Staircase in the Würzburg Residence, Würzburg, 1735

Basilica of the Fourteen Holy Helpers, Bad Staffelstein, 1743–1772

09

CLAUDE-NICOLAS LEDOUX

With his progressive social and architectural ideas, Claude-Nicolas Ledoux, who appreciated classical literature and preferred to describe himself as an architect philosopher, was among architecture's most imaginative representatives.

CLAUDE-NICOLAS LEDOUX

This French architect first learned his trade in Paris; his teacher, Jacques François Blondel, was a champion of Neo-Classicism. His first job, in local government, took Ledoux out of the capital.

In the provinces of Burgundy and Champagne his responsibilities covered the construction of bridges, schools and transport routes, as well as farming matters and farmers' living conditions. At the same time, the young architect made the acquaintance of high administrative officials, from whose ranks many of his later commissions came. When in 1764 Ledoux married the daughter of a court musician, his connections were definitively established: exchanging his administrative work for numerous commissions from the court, he could now settle in the capital and start building for the Paris nobility.

Ledoux's approach was eclectic, and he sometimes quoted from classical antiquity, at other times from the Italian Renaissance or French Neo-Classicism. In his façade for the Hôtel d'Uzès, for example, he employed the Baroque, while for the Hotel d'Halwyll he drew upon Neo-Classicism.

In 1771 the 35-year-old Ledoux was engaged to build a saltworks in the east of the country. Between Arc and Senans, near Besançon, he created the Saline du Roi, construction began in 1774. Ledoux was not satisfied with a simple factory; he designed an entire ideal town for working people. Processing areas and workshops were to be grouped in a semicircle around the house of the director, and these in turn were surrounded by houses and public buildings, such as churches and communal baths. Only part of his design was realized, but this already demonstrates the concept behind it: living and working were to be closely linked. Simple geometric forms such as cubes, spheres and pyramids determined the design of the buildings. The saltworks began operating in 1779, and more than 250 workers lived in Ledoux's houses. He continued to dedicate himself to his ideal city, but many of his "speaking buildings," expressing utopian ideals in Neo-Classical forms, were never executed.

With the outbreak of the French Revolution, Ledoux's public and private commissions dried up; in 1793, the former royal architect even spent a short time in prison. During his last years, he devoted himself to his writings on architectural theory, the first (and only) volume appearing two years before his death.

Saline Royale, Arc-et-Senans, 1774–1779

10

THOMAS JEFFERSON

In the newly founded United States, architecture largely followed European styles. It was the buildings of classical Rome that inspired master builders, and so both private and public buildings exhibited temple façades, columned entrance halls, and elegant domes. Jefferson was among these enthusiastic builders.

THOMAS JEFFERSON

1743 Born April 13, in Albemarle County, Virginia
1760–1767
Earns degree in law and begins practice as an attorney
1772 Marries Martha Wayles Skelton
1774 Serves as a delegate from Virginia to congress; prepares the Declaration of Independence for the colonies
1779–81
Serves as governor of Virginia
1786 Signs a declaration on religious freedom
1796 Becomes vice president
1801–09
Serves as the third president of the United States
1825 The University of Virginia opens its doors
1826 Dies July 4, in Monticello, Virginia

Thomas Jefferson, lawyer, politician, and architect, built his country house, Monticello, in the middle of an old tobacco plantation at the gates of the little town of Charlottesville. On this "little mountain" one could imagine oneself suddenly transplanted to a time several centuries ago. The portal of this residence already resembles the front of a temple; mighty columns support a profiled cornice on which rests a classical pediment. At the rear, too, a similar portico leads into the building. Projecting side wings are set back from the prominent porch, and the house is crowned by a central dome. For his new building, Jefferson made use of European architectural models, such as the Roman Pantheon, but also a masterwork of Renaissance architecture, the Villa Rotonda, which itself was based on classical buildings. This central-plan building, which had been built well over 200 years earlier near Vicenza in Italy by Andrea Palladio, was the American's chief inspiration, above all as concerns of the design of the façade.

Jefferson's comfortable countryseat was only the beginning of his career as an architect. As his next project, Jefferson took on the seat of government of his home state, Virginia. In its capital, Richmond, he built the Virginia State Capitol. Anyone who had expected modern architecture for the young nation must have had quite a surprise. On a hill above the city, from 1785 a classical temple began to arise, its declared model this time being a temple from Roman times, the Maison Carrée in Nîmes, in the south of France.

Politicians gathered there for the first time after seven years of building. At the very top of the agenda for the delegates and Governor Jefferson were topics such as the abolition of feudal privileges, the separation of church and state, and establishing of a public education system. The latter was energetically taken in hand by Jefferson himself; after his term of office as third president of the United States had come to an end, he built and financed the University of Virginia, designing an entire "academic village." For each of the ten faculties to be taught he designed a separate pavilion, which contained teaching and residential areas. In designing the library, Jefferson seems to have once again had the Pantheon in mind; an impressive dome adorns the building and provides daylight. In March 1825 the first 123 students began their studies in Virginia. Jefferson also concerned himself with their physical well being, and several of them enjoyed Sunday dinner in the ex-president's house. Among the students there were some of the finest minds of the young nation, including the founder of detective fiction, Edgar Allan Poe.

Monticello, near Charlottesville, 1769–1808

11

KARL FRIEDRICH SCHINKEL

One of the most prolific German architects of the first half of the 19th century, Karl Friedrich Schinkel created more than 150 buildings in Germany and Poland, most of which are still to be seen today. He was also an accomplished painter, stage set designer, and interior decorator.

His career proceeded rapidly; as early as 1815, in his mid-30s, he was appointed chief building advisor and was given important commissions, including the construction of a guardhouse for the royal palace. After the theater in the center of Berlin, in the Gendarmenmarkt, had burned down, the king's choice fell once again on the master builder from Brandenburg. Its replacement, built from 1818 to 1821, represents one of Schinkel's masterworks. The worthy framework for the new theater was already in place: the symmetrically designed square could already boast two church buildings close by, the German and the French cathedrals. The Schauspielhaus in the center of the Gendarmenmarkt welcomes visitors with its classical, well-proportioned forms, more precisely with a Greek temple frontage built according to all the rules of the textbooks. In the interior of the building, the design strictly follows the law of fitness for purpose. Schinkel made no secret of his motto: "In architecture everything must be true, all masking or disguising of the structure is a fault." The theater was opened with a production of Mozart's opera *The Magic Flute*. The sets were designed by the great music-lover Friedrich Schinkel.

With his references to the architecture of classical antiquity, Schinkel was following a current trend. In the late 18th century, both clients and architects saw in the temples of classical Greece the epitome of perfect beauty and thus the model for contemporary architecture. Accordingly, it was Schinkel's buildings in the Neo-Classical style that met with the greatest approval, above all the Old Museum in the Lustgarten. A flight of stairs leads into the building, which, with its rotunda as a central hall, also alludes to the Roman Pantheon. But Schinkel was perfectly capable of enthusiasm for other eras. In building the Friedrichswerder church in Berlin, for example, he was alluding to medieval Gothic. Schloss Kamenz in Silesia is likewise reminiscent of a medieval castle, and other designs demonstrate Schinkel's weakness for the Romantic. Not only with regard to his building assignments, but also in respect of his models, Friedrich Schinkel shows himself to have always been open to the old—and to the new.

Konzerthaus, Berlin, 1818–1821

Old Museum, Berlin, 1822–1829

12

GOTTFRIED SEMPER

Before he decided to study mathematics, Gottfried Semper chose a career as a professional army officer. Even when he finally studied architecture, his enthusiasm for it was still muted. Yet he was to have a profound impact on German architecture.

GOTTFRIED SEMPER

Born in Hamburg, Semper was initially drawn to foreign lands. In Paris he again took up the study of architecture, and this time it clearly took hold of him. In southern Europe he traveled to the classical temples and studied their coloration. Fascinated by the interplay of the arts of architecture, painting and sculpture, Semper presented his findings from Italy and Greece in book form.

As soon as this project was completed, the 31-year-old was appointed to a professorship in architecture, and in 1834 he began teaching at the Dresden Academy. With his approach of linking theory and practice, Semper was striking out on new paths. At the same time, the teacher and author was given his first major project: his design for the Dresden Court Theater had been approved, and he began work in 1838. Having a semicircular form, and being integrated into the existing Baroque backdrop of buildings, the theater caused a sensation. Semper now began to receive commissions from all over Germany: his adoption of the Renaissance style had immediately found admirers.

Semper sympathized with revolutionary ideas, and so after the uprisings of 1848 had been quashed he fled to Paris. Over the decades that followed, one move succeeded another; failing as a German to get a foothold in France, he moved on to London. There too he had hardly any opportunity to make his mark as an architect, and so he resumed his work as a professor. Now aged 52, in the hope of supplementing his teaching work with building commissions, he took advantage of an offer from Switzerland. He had to remain patient for a little longer, but in 1860 he was finally able to go ahead with the building of the Polytechnikum in Zurich. Further commissions, and not only from Switzerland, followed. At the same time, Semper consolidated his reputation as an architectural theorist with his influential publication *Style*. A further success involved yet another move: Semper's designs for the Kaiserforum on the Ringstrasse in Vienna were accepted. The master builder now settled in Vienna and began work on the great building complex of museums and Burgtheater, which however was subjected to myriad alterations after his death.

Semperoper, Dresden, 1871–1878

13

OTTO WAGNER

"Nothing that is not useful can be beautiful"—architect Otto Wagner didn't let pragmatism stand in the way of imagination, whether it was a fine town house or stations on the Vienna urban railway system, his styles encompassed Renaissance revival to avant-garde Modernism.

OTTO WAGNER

1841   Born July 13, in Penzing near Vienna, Austria

1857–59
Studies at the Vienna Polytechnic Institute

1860–63
Studies at the Academy of Art, Vienna

1864   Harmonietheater and 12 residential buildings in the Harmoniegasse and Wasagasse, Vienna

1875   Further residential houses in Vienna: in Hauptstrasse, Bauernmarkt, and Schönburggasse

1882–84
Länderbank, Vienna

1894   Becomes a professor at the Vienna Academy

1899   Becomes a member of the Vienna Secession

1918   Dies April 11, in Vienna

When Otto Wagner took up his first commissions, he was still enthusiastic about revivalism; like many of his contemporaries, he borrowed from a number of architectural traditions. His preference was for the Renaissance era, as shown in the façade of the house at 23 Schottenring, which Wagner built in 1877, on the Ringstrasse in Vienna. But he and his clients were also enthusiastic about Baroque forms. A mere three decades later, he had shelved the return to earlier traditions. Now he spoke of Vienna as the "birthplace of the art of our time."

Wagner's move from revivalism to Modernism did not take place in a vacuum. Vienna had become the fourth largest city in Europe, and many buildings were under construction: the new metropolis was being given a modern face. The Ringstrasse, which was being built at this time, was edged by some 850 impressive edifices, public and private palaces. And right in the middle of Viennese Modernism, as the two decades around 1900 were known, Otto Wagner built museums, academies, parliament buildings, and public monuments. By the turn of the century, his greatest project was the design of the Vienna Stadtbahn, the urban rail network.

From 1894, Wagner, a government building advisor and professor of architecture, showed himself to be open to new ideas. For his many designs for railway stations and bridges he placed iron, always lacquered in green, in prominent positions. Curving lines and ornamentation recalling foliage show his interest in Art Nouveau. In 1899, already 60 years old, he joined the Vienna Secessionists, a group of visual artists who rejected the revival of past times.

Thus no trace of revivalism was to be found in the Viennese Post Office Savings Bank, one of Wagner's masterworks, built between 1904 and 1906, in the center of Vienna. The exterior is clad in granite and marble panels, supported by aluminum bolts—a new material, like the reinforced concrete that was also used. The center of the building is the banking hall, above which stretches a glass barrel vault. The entire interior of the Savings Bank was also designed by Wagner in the same clear and rational way. His unprecedented designs were very influential, and among the successors of this architect, urban planner, furniture designer, and theorist was, not least, Adolf Loos, who ultimately maintained that all decorative ornamentation was "a crime."

Austrian Postal Savings Bank, Vienna, 1904–1906

Austrian Postal Savings Bank, Vienna, 1904–1906

Majolika House at the Wienzeile (Vienna Row), Vienna, 1898–1899

14

DANIEL BURNHAM

Daniel Hudson Burnham started working in an architects' office in Chicago, where his professional future was sealed when he met his future business partner there, John Wellborn Root.

DANIEL BURNHAM

1846 Born September 4, in Henderson, New York

1889–91 Monadnock Building, Chicago

1890–95 Reliance Building, Chicago

1891 Masonic Temple, Chicago

1893 Becomes chief architect of the Chicago World's Fair

1895 Reliance Building, Chicago

1901–02 Designs for the District of Columbia

1902 Flatiron Building, New York

1906–09 Urban planning designs for Chicago

1912 Dies June 1, in Heidelberg, Germany

The two architects complemented each other wonderfully: Daniel Burnham was considered the pragmatist, while Root was esteemed for his wealth of invention. Together the pair built a significant proportion of the architecture that has become known as the Chicago School.

In the last quarter of the 19th century, the first skyscrapers began to shoot up in Chicago. Above all in the Loop, the rapidly growing business district of the city, where there was a shortage of building land, and only upwards was there no restriction on space. Between 1889 and 1891, Burnham and Root added the Monadnock Building to the ever more imposing skyline. The building was 17 stories high, making it the largest office building of its time. Thick walls still formed the supporting elements of the building, but with the next project the architects were already exploring new techniques. In 1890 they began the Reliance Building, whose 61 meters of height combine steel, terracotta and, principally glass. When Root died in 1891, Charles A. Atwood took over his role on this project, and it is on his designs that the more open façade of the upper floors is based. Unlike the ground and first floor, it is decorated with ornamentation and designed in a more transparent way. Characteristic, notably are the so-called Chicago windows, which are inset into the frame structure. They consist of a large glass pane flanked by two narrow panes that can be opened.

Burnham & Company continued to celebrate their successes. Their Masonic Temple with its 22 stories was even—though only for a short time—the tallest building in the world. In 1893 Daniel Burnham became chief architect of the Chicago World's Fair.

Burnham left his lasting mark on the cityscape not only in Chicago, but also in New York. The site on the corner of Broadway and Fifth Avenue in the heart of Manhattan seemed hardly suitable for building on: it was not only narrow in the extreme but triangular. Yet the ground plan seems to have inspired Daniel Burnham, who used the available surface area in a positively exemplary manner. The Fuller Building, which he built there in 1902, was one of New York's first high-rise buildings. The 20-stories high building is better known as the Flatiron Building, a nickname it owes to its ground-plan form, which does indeed look like that of a pressing iron. Built in the form of a metal skeleton, the building towers up to 91 metres, with the framework concealed by the terracotta façade and not recognizable from the outside.

The Flatiron Building was not able to claim the title of the tallest building in the world, but even today it can easily defend its status as an architectural icon.

Flatiron Building, New York City, 1902

15 ANTONI GAUDÍ

With his rejection of straight lines and symmetrical ground plans, Antoni Gaudí opened a new chapter in the architectural history of Barcelona. With their strong colors and glittering façades, it is his highly imaginative designs that still characterize this Spanish port.

ANTONI GAUDÍ

The son of a coppersmith, Gaudí began his architectural career on a not exactly promising note: he left university with the lowest possible grade, a "pass." However, private clients had confidence in his skill—to such an extent that this unconventional architect was soon inundated with commissions. His sources of inspiration were unusual: he was passionate about both medieval Gothic and Moorish architecture, to which he alluded when building the Casa Vicens. This home of a brickyard owner fascinates in particular by its wealth of contrasts: small turrets on the roof are reminiscent of the minarets of mosques, and patterns of colorfully glazed tiles encompass the entire façade.

The young architect soon found his most important client in the industrialist Eusebi Güell, for whom he first built a palatial residence, adorning its roof with a whole forest of fantastic chimneys. But Güell had greater things in mind; he dreamt of a garden city, whose houses on a steep cliff were to offer a view of the Mediterranean. While Güell's plan did not find widespread acceptance and only two residential buildings were finally executed, Gaudí tackled his part of the work and transformed a 20-hectare area in the north of Barcelona into a walk-in sculpture. Between pine and palm trees, mosaics of glass and ceramics sparkle on the steps, benches, and houses of Park Güell.

"The straight line is the line of Man, the curve is the line of God"—this was Gaudí's fundamental belief. His masterwork, a church known as the Sagrada Família, was designed entirely according to this principle. When the 31-year-old took over the construction of this church, a crypt was already being built. Gaudí only briefly followed the existing Gothic forms, however. Soon he had found his model for the basic framework: nature itself. With their "branches," the pillars and supports look like trees. The Sagrada Família, as a church of atonement, was to be built exclusively from donated funds, which the master builder frequently supplied in person. Finally he realized that this task allowed him no time for further projects, and in 1914 he decided to devote himself exclusively to the church. The builders' hut became his new home. But when the architect died in 1926 after a tram accident, this "sermon in stone" was still far from completion. Of the three façades, only the eastern one had been begun, not to speak of the bell towers, the tallest of which was to grow to 170 meters. Even today, Gaudí's masterpiece primarily presents itself as a building site—although this hardly detracts from its overwhelming impact.

Sagrada Família, Barcelona, 1882–2026 (anticipated completion)

Casa Batlló, Barcelona, 1904–1906

Park Güell, Barcelona, 1900–1914

16 LOUIS SULLIVAN

With his plans for high-rise buildings in the Chicago of the 1890s, Louis Sullivan declared himself a revolutionary. His approach was very simple: a skyscraper, he declared, "must be tall, every inch of it tall. The force and power of altitude must be in it, the glory and pride of exaltation must be in it."

LOUIS SULLIVAN

1856 Born September 3, in Boston

1879 Works with Dankmar Adler, Chicago

1886–89 Auditorium Building, Chicago, with Adler

1891 Wainwright Building, St. Louis

1896 Guarantee Building, Buffalo, with Adler

1899 Marries Margaret Hattabough

1899–1904 Schlesinger & Mayer Store, Chicago (now Carson, Pirie & Scott Building)

1924 Dies April 14, in Chicago

1946 Awarded the Gold Medal of the American Institute of Architects

That architecture was to be his field was at first less than clear, however. Louis Sullivan twice took up an academic career. Born in Boston, he first studied in his home city, but left the Institute of Technology after only a year. Neither did he stay long at the Académie des Beaux-Arts in Paris. Back in Chicago, he was primarily active as an interior decorator. But it was not to be long before, in his mid-20s, that the son of a Swiss mother and an Irish dance teacher finally found his métier and his place, in the heart of Chicago.

After great areas of the city had been destroyed by the Great Chicago Fire, in 1871, rebuilding proceeded at top gear. For the first time, architects resorted to a new construction method: rather than building thick walls to support the weight of the building, they constructed load-bearing frameworks of steel. Over the years that followed, business and office high-rises of metal and glass shot up into the air. And many of them were Sullivan's. From 1880 he worked in the office of the architect Dankmar Adler. The two executed their commissions for office buildings and department stores with a very clear division of labor: Adler was the engineer, Sullivan the designer. The combination worked well, and a first major commission was the building of the opera house, incorporated into a ten-story building. The trend took off, and in 1890–1891 the two architects designed their first skyscraper with a steel skeleton, the Wainwright Building. More skyscrapers followed. The Guaranty Building, built in Buffalo by Adler & Sullivan up to 1895, by no means disguised its height in the façade; the vertical is clearly emphasized in the surface of decorative terracotta.

Sullivan's conviction was that a building's structure, function, and appearance should form a harmonious whole. Architectural decoration could certainly play its part, but it should be subordinate to function. With the Schlesinger & Mayer Store (today Carson, Pirie & Scott), constructed between 1899 and 1904, Sullivan provided a fine example of this principle. The two lower floors of the building show his weakness for rich ornamentation. In the tower-like extension of one corner of the building is the entrance to the store, richly decorated with wrought iron. From the third story, the situation looks different, however: the building's load-bearing metal framework is clearly apparent, and the windows are set well back behind the steel framework. The extent of the stories as horizontal elements is as strongly emphasized as the vertical lines. This creates a cell-like structure on the surface of the building. Unlike many high-rise buildings, the Schlesinger & Mayer Store has a curved main corner above the main entrance.

Carson Pirie Scott Building, Chicago, 1899–1904

17

VICTOR HORTA

As a young architect, Victor Horta set new standards in the villa built for Émile Tassel: it is one of the first residential buildings in Europe in the Art Nouveau style. Horta was soon in demand for his daring ideas, and in his chosen home, Brussels, Horta left behind many luxurious private houses.

VICTOR HORTA

1861 Born January 6, in Ghent, Belgium

From 1881
Studies at the Académie des Beaux-Arts, Brussels

1893 Villa Tassel

1895 Commissioned to design the headquarters of the Belgian Socialist Party (Maison du Peuple)

From 1897
Teaches at the Free University in Brussels

1897–1900
Villa van Eetvelde

1903 Grand Bazar Anspach

1912–31
Teaches at the Académie des Beaux-Arts, Brussels

1947 Dies September 8, in Brussels

Educated in Ghent, Paris, and Brussels, Victor Horta led an independent life from his mid-20s. His ideas were revolutionary. Replacing wood with iron was his first move, although it was not so much the material that was new as the place where it was used. Horta used it, for example, for the entrance hall of the house that he built for Tassel: slender iron components continue in the form of tendril-like ornamentation on floor, walls, and ceiling—and, not least, the iron columns themselves take up the vegetal motifs. Everything seems to be in movement, linked together by whirls and curves. The arrangement of rooms and passages too is determined by flowing transitions.

While Horta transposed the vocabulary of Art Nouveau with its curved lines and vegetal ornament in the Tassel house, his next major commission proved to be quite different. The newly founded Belgian Socialist Party commissioned the still quite unknown architect to design its assembly building. Horta envisaged a palace, "which would not be a palace at all, but a 'house,' in which light and air represent the luxury that was for so long denied to the miserable living quarters of the workers." The curved façade of this early major work by Horta formed a framework of slender iron elements. Brickwork played only a subsidiary role in the Maison du Peuple—the foreground was dominated by large areas of glass. The building attracted enormous attention, a situation that was to be repeated when the house was demolished in 1965 in the face of all protests.

Horta's later designs were no longer designed for such specific purposes, and even the target group changed. Over the years that followed, Horta created two large department stores and in particular urban villas for wealthy entrepreneurs. It was precisely the latter who posed a particular problem for the architect: how could the narrow but tall town houses typical of Brussels, constricted within long rows, be made visually larger? Horta had the good fortune to have a largely free hand in realizing his ideas; thanks to glass roofs, his buildings give the impression of being flooded with light, and mirrors placed opposite each other suggest whole series of rooms.

In the urban villa executed by Horta at the turn of the century for the wealthy manufacturer Solvay, he indulged to its height his weakness for moving forms in the curved façade, whose bow fronts are vaulted. The interior welcomes the visitor in a flood of light, rooms merge into each other, walls and ceiling of the first floor are broken up into skillfully structured glass surfaces. Horta concerned himself not only with the overall structure of the building, but also with the décor and furnishings down to the smallest detail.

Staircase Hôtel Tassel, Brussels, 1893

Horta Museum, view into the salon, Brussel, 1898–1901

Staircase in the Hôtel van Eetvelde, Brussels, 1895–1900

18 FRANK LLOYD WRIGHT

Frank Lloyd Wright spent 72 of his 92 years as an architect. Unlike many of his colleagues, this devoted family man primarily built houses. This focus did not, however, prevent him from designing one of the best-known museum buildings in the world: The Solomon R. Guggenheim Museum in New York.

FRANK LLOYD WRIGHT

1867 Born June 8, in Richland Center, Wisconsin

1887 Begins work in the architectural office of Louis Henry Sullivan and Dankmar Adler in Chicago

1893 The Winslow House Wright, his first independent commission

1916–20 Hotel Imperial in Tokyo with Antonin Raymond

1936–37 Falling Water House in Bear Run, Pennsylvania

1936–39 Johnson Building in Racine, Wisconsin

1956–59 Guggenheim Museum, New York

1959 Dies April 9, in Phoenix, Arizona

For his plans, Wright at an early stage chose the keyword "organic." Organic architecture fits into its context—into its natural surroundings, and into its time. A new building in the 20th century, the young architect concluded, should not imitate anything old, but should reflect the present with modern materials and new technology. Wright adopted one further principle: the standard for his buildings was the human being, whose needs determined his designs. Thus the father of six children designed for his own home in Oak Park, Chicago, an enormous playroom with child-friendly low windows, wide window seats and, above all, plenty of room. Residential houses, and by no means exclusively those in the luxury bracket, remained Wright's primary task.

For Wright, a building seemed in harmony with its surroundings when in, fitted in, as well as possible, into its specific natural environment. His "prairie houses," for example, were designed against the background of the endless horizontals of the open prairies of the Midwest. The three-story Fallingwater House takes the harmony between building and landscape to the limit: walls and floors are of wood and natural stone, while the ceilings, traversed by glass courses, allow nature to enter the interior. Seen from the outside, the waterfall that gives the house its name seems to arise from within the house itself, so perfectly does it fit into the landscape.

Wright's rejection of detail is found in the open, generously flowing room designs that he presented in 1943 to the industrialist Solomon Guggenheim, who was looking for suitable spaces in New York for his collection of abstract art. The building that finally took shape on Fifth Avenue—the Solomon R. Guggenheim Museum—in the middle of Manhattan was described by some critics as a "washing machine." But Wright was not deterred. His Guggenheim Museum looks like an ivory-colored sculpture. On the modest substructure rests a stack of round discs, whose diameters increase as we move upwards. In the interior, a spiral ramp winds along the outer wall from the ground floor up to the top story; visitors, Wright said, should first to go up the top of the building in the elevator and from there explore the artworks step by step as they move downwards. It was not just critics and fellow architects who voiced concerns: artists wondered how their works could be shown to effect on the curved walls of the building. It was clear at the opening that they had no reason for doubt. Sadly, Frank Lloyd Wright was not able to enjoy the success of his extraordinary building, dying only a few months before the completion of this architectural icon.

Fallingwater House in Bear Run, Pennsylvania, 1935–1937

Solomon R. Guggenheim Museum, New York City, 1943–1959

Staircase in the Solomon R. Guggenheim Museum, New York City, 1943–1959

19

AUGUSTE PERRET

In the early 20th century, Auguste Perret discovered a still recent building material, reinforced concrete. Delighting in its clear, elementary forms, he used it in hundreds of innovative designs over the following decades.

AUGUSTE PERRET

Perret was barely 30 years old when he created a new building in the Rue Franklin in Paris, a building that soon made history. The young architect made no secret of the structure of this apartment building: the load-bearing reinforced concrete skeleton is clearly separated from the non-load-bearing filling and both are clearly visible in the façade. Thanks to the narrow supports and large window areas, the building, despite its size, does not appear at all massive, but rather light and transparent.

Perret had decided in favor of a comparatively new building material: reinforced concrete, in other words concrete cast over a framework of iron bars, which had been in use only since the mid-19th century. Perret remained loyal to the material all his life, and it is the main element of his buildings of the decades that followed. Only rarely are the façades of his concrete structures disguised with cladding, as with the Théâtre des Champs-Elysées, which is adorned with reliefs by the artist Antoine Bourdelle. This site for contemporary music on the impressive Paris street, incidentally, became talked about not only from an architectural point of view—it was there, after all, that modernism in ballet originated.

Perret, who from 1905 worked with his brothers Gustave and Claude, moved straight on to the next commissions, his chosen material continuing to be among the tools of his trade. This is shown by some 380 executed designs. He created department stores, urban villas, cathedrals and museums in concrete—in Casablanca, Paris, and São Paulo. His work soon found its way into exhibitions and architectural journals, and Perret, who was also active

as a teacher (not least among his pupils was Le Corbusier), was honored with many awards. Self-confident, dignified, and elegant—this was how his colleagues described him. There was one more thing on which they all agreed: Perret was a man of few words. His eloquence was expressed in his designs.

In France, though not in his much-loved Paris, but in Le Havre in Normandy, Perret made his name as a town planner. From 1945 he dedicated himself to the reconstruction of the port, which had been almost completely destroyed during the Second World War. Within ten years the new Le Havre came into being, according to the plans produced by his office, with concrete appearing everywhere, and used not just for basic utilitarian buildings. His prefabricated private houses, the church of St. Joseph, and the Town Hall have a special fascination all of their own, and since 2005 have been placed on UNESCO's list of World Cultural Heritage sites.

Le Havre City Hall, 1952–1958

20

WALTER GROPIUS

It was on industrial buildings that Gropius, born in Berlin, founded his reputation. In the more than five decades of his creative career he went on to extend his field of operations considerably, and devoted himself to social housing as much as to high-rise designs. Above all, his name is linked with the Bauhaus in Dessau.

WALTER GROPIUS

1883 Born May 18, in Berlin, Germany

1903–07
Studies at the colleges of technology in Munich and Berlin

1907–10
Works as an assistant to Peter Behrens in Berlin

1910 Becomes an independent architect

1919 Appointed to the College of Visual Arts in Weimar, renamed the Bauhaus

1928 Gives up his post of director of the Bauhaus; opens his own office in Berlin

1919–30
Siemensstadt, Berlin

1937 Appointed to teach architecture at Harvard University

1969 Dies July 5, in Boston

Beginnings are often difficult, and this was certainly true of Walter Gropius: "I am not capable of drawing a straight line," he wrote to his mother when he was a student. But his lack of talent as a draughtsman could not hold him back for long: after completing his studies and after only a few years working with Peter Behrens, Gropius, still aged only 20, received his first major commission: to build a factory. From 1911 he worked on this project, the Fagus factory, with Adolf Meyer in the small town of Alfeld an der Leine in Lower Saxony. The modern materials of glass and metal determined the image of the building, which is reduced to a compact and at the same time transparent cube: only in places are the glass surfaces broken up by areas of wall. In the corners, the two architects rejected the addition of supports, increasing the light and fragile impression created by the building, which also does without pediments. The only decoration of the flat-roofed building are the vertical and horizontal lines with which the façade is uniformly covered.

With this factory building, Gropius had created a masterpiece. He continued to work in the same plain and unpretentious style, his cubical structures determined by clear, white surfaces and severely symmetrical rows of windows. For Gropius, a priority was "that artistic design should not be a matter of luxury, but must be the business of life itself." Thus many of his designs even for social housing seem severe. Economically priced building meant for Gropius the use of standardized and prefabricated components, put together on the principle of the construction kit. That such mass production did not necessarily meet the taste of the masses was shown by the criticism of his residential high-rise houses and workers' settlements, including Gropius City in Berlin.

It is above all the Bauhaus with which his name is linked. Walter Gropius was a cofounder and first director of the school of arts and crafts in Weimar, which opened its doors in 1919. Artists, craftworkers, and later also architects worked hand in hand there. When the Bauhaus moved to Dessau, Gropius planned the new school building, or rather "the new building of the future." Between 1925 and 1926, three L-shaped wings took shape, linked to each other. The right one accommodated the workshop; the Bauhaus logo is displayed in large lettering on the glazed façade of the four-story building. Wide window areas also characterize the connecting area. The students' block, however, corresponding to the individuality within, is designed with balconies and single windows. After the completion of the students' block, Gropius tackled the living quarters of the Bauhaus teachers, and a whole settlement took shape. Under the Nazi regime, the Bauhaus was violently criticized and finally closed down. In 1937 its creator emigrated to England and in 1937 moved on to Cambridge, Massachusetts, where he taught architecture at Harvard University.

Staircase in the Bauhaus Dessau, 1926–1928

Fagus Factory, Alfeld, 1911–1913

21

LUDWIG MIES VAN DER ROHE

One of the most influential architects of the 20th century, Ludwig Mies van der Rohe rejected an academic education. He learned his craft in the office of Peter Behrens—one of his fellow-students there being Le Corbusier.

LUDWIG MIES VAN DER ROHE

1886 Born March 27, in Aachen, Germany

1913 Opens his own office in Steglitz, Germany

1926 Becomes vice president of the Deutscher Werkbund

1927 Weissenhof Settlement, Stuttgart

1930–33
Serves as director of the Bauhaus

1938 Emigrates to the US; becomes director of the Illinois Institute of Technology, Chicago

1951 Residential high-rise at 860–880 Lake Shore Drive, Chicago

1958 Seagram Building, New York

1962–68
New National Gallery, Berlin

1969 Dies August 17, in Chicago

Office buildings and exhibition pavilions, factories and museums, private houses and libraries, in the six decades of his career, Mies van der Rohe continually discovered new challenges, whether in Berlin, Chicago, New York, or Stuttgart.

True to his motto that "only today can be given form," in 1927 he assumed the artistic direction of the Weissenhof Settlement in Stuttgart. Nothing less was presented there than the future of building, on the occasion of the exhibition *Die Wohnung*. The principles Mies van der Rohe and 16 other architects had adopted were made clear by this "model settlement": the 21 houses, containing 63 apartments under flat roofs, were bare of decoration. The enthusiasm of public and press was muted, and even their fellow architects were critical: "In multifarious horizontal terraces, uninhabitably crowded together, a heaping of low-lying cubes throngs up a hillside, reminiscent rather of a suburb of Jerusalem than of apartments for Stuttgart … an Arab village."

In 1929 he created for the Spanish port of Barcelona an exhibition pavilion that demonstrated his continuing development of Bauhaus architecture. Here architecture has been reduced to absolute basics: a few plain walls and a large, flat roof. The free-standing steel pillars and the stone walls are mirrored in two pools of water, while interior and exterior space are linked rather than separated by large areas of glass.

Rectangular forms, flat roofs, transparency—the architect continued to be true to his clear, rationalistic building concepts. In 1938 he emigrated to the United States. There, together with Herbert Greenwald, he created large residential high-rise complexes, such as the apartment houses on Lake Shore Drive in Chicago. Reduced to a structural skeleton, these buildings are pure steel constructions, with extensively glazed façades. As early as 1923 the Berlin-born Mies had clarified his views on modern office architecture: "The materials are concrete, iron, glass. Reinforced concrete buildings are skeleton buildings by their nature. Neither pastry nor armored tanks." The Seagram Building, completed in 1958 on New York's Park Avenue, the architect's first office high-rise, also speaks volumes in this respect. Mies van der Rohe's office towers at the same time fit harmoniously into the urban space that surrounds them—the glass fronts of the lower stories merge seamlessly into the squares around them.

Seagram Building, New York City, 1955–1958

Barcelona Pavilion, Barcelona, 1929 (1986 reconstruction)

22

LE CORBUSIER

He wrote more than 30 books on art and architecture, painted and drew, and devoted himself to poetry and furniture making. But Le Corbusier would become famous for his buildings: the Swiss-born architect made a name for himself on three continents during the six decades of his career.

LE CORBUSIER

Charles-Édouard Jeanneret, son of a pianist and a mountaineer, began his career as an architect early in life. In his early 20s he worked in the office of the architect Auguste Perret in Paris, and two years later he worked as a draughtsman in the studio of Peter Behrens. In 1914 the young architect and urban planner entered the field of the serial production of houses, developing over the decades a rationalized method of building that he employed in the design of his new home in Paris. From 1920, Jeanneret started calling himself Le Corbusier.

He made a start with the "Domino" system, based on a standardized framework of reinforced concrete, to which the client in question could add walls, windows or doors from an architectural catalogue. In line with Citroën's mechanized car production, the Swiss architect then worked on the "Citrohan" house. He made no secret of his enthusiasm for new technologies and media.

But his ideas on the city of the future did not meet with unalloyed approval. Le Corbusier's rejection of traditional city planning also found its impassioned critics—a glance at his "machine for living" in Marseille will show why. From 1945, in the south of the French Mediterranean city, he created the Unité de l'Habitation, a high-rise complex that consists not only of apartments but also shops and offices. Almost the whole urban infrastructure is present there, for it was intended that its residents need never leave their self-contained concrete "village."

And it was not only his urban planning designs that demonstrate Le Corbusier's enthusiasm for concrete as a building material. It was as a "concrete pile" that his project on a high plateau above the village of Ronchamp became known. In 1950, in this hilly district some 20 kilometers from Belfort, the architect began to build a pilgrimage chapel, which was to replace the previous, destroyed structure. Notre-Dame-du-Haut was to offer space for about 200 believers, but also be able to receive the swarms of pilgrims who streamed to this site twice a year. Le Corbusier provided them a space with an exterior choir in front of the east wall, sheltered by the widely projecting brown roof. The problem of space was thus solved in the best possible way. So is everything else right angles and straight sides, arranged in neat symmetrical order? Not quite, or at any rate not only: a windowless tower and an arched white wall, on which rests a bulging, heavy roof, determine our first impression of the chapel. Only on the north wall do right angles dominate, while the west wall is rounded off. Various large openings are distributed as though at random over the façade that frames the main entrance. Partly covered with plaster, partly exposing the concrete beneath, this design by Le Corbusier also inspired critics to invent various nicknames, but the "sacred garage" nevertheless ended up as a milestone of modern architecture.

Chapel of Notre Dame du Haut, Ronchamp, 1950–1955

Unité d'Habitation, Marseille, 1947–1952

Saint-Pierre, Firminy, 1970–2006

23

GERRIT RIETVELD

The Dutch architect and designer Gerrit Rietveld began his career early: as a twelve year old he entered his father's furniture workshop. At first his interest was in the applied arts, but it was not long before he was also fascinated by architecture.

GERRIT RIETVELD

To begin with, he seems to have been influenced by painting. In 1918 he designed an armchair made from wooden slats, whose reduced forms are reminiscent of the paintings of abstract artists. But in addition to this, in the years that followed color took on ever greater importance in his furniture designs. Red, yellow, and blue contrast with black, white, and gray: in this way Rietveld's armchair developed into the Red-Blue Chair, which brought international recognition to the designer from Utrecht. The reduced palette incidentally corresponded to the colors that were used by the painters of the group De Stijl. It was from this group too, with whose members he was in touch from 1919, that Rietveld was to adopt his asymmetrical designs. This is seen, for example, in his Berlin Chair, which looks more like a sculpture than a piece of furniture. Rietveld also became prominent as a typographer, and he designed many printed items both on his own account and for others. In the late 1920s and above all the 1930s he developed furniture for mass production and as an architect also resorted to prefabricated building parts. For his *kernwoningen* (housing modules) in Utrecht and Vienna he relied on mass production for all the essential components.

While little is still preserved of his later residential building projects, his main work long ago became an architectural icon. In 1924 Truus Schröder-Schräder commissioned Rietveld, until then hardly known as an architect, to build a private house for her. His 35-year-old client was looking for a new home for herself and her three children after the death of her husband. When she could not find a suitable property to rent, Rietveld finally tendered successfully for a new building at the edge of the city of Utrecht. Following Schröder's ideas, Rietveld designed a small but revolutionary house. His client wanted to see walls only where they were indispensable; what was important to her was the view of the landscape and the practicality of the whole design. Rietveld met her wishes with movable walls on the first floor, which offered the flexibility requested by his demanding client. Other areas, such as the kitchen and a den on the ground floor, were separated from the living quarters. Due to cost, Rietveld refrained from executing the entire structure in concrete as originally planned, but used this material only for the foundations and balconies. A skylight and generously cut windows allow light into the house, whose façades are structured by further horizontal and vertical elements.

Rietveld Schröder House, Utrecht, 1924

24

RICHARD NEUTRA

The impact of the Viennese-born Richard Neutra can be seen in southern California. His many private houses and villas from Los Angeles to Palm Springs are designed on a grand scale and yet at the same time are impressively integrated into their natural environment.

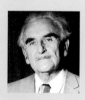

RICHARD NEUTRA

During his studies in architecture at the Technische Hochschule in Vienna, Neutra was strongly influenced by the work of the architect Adolf Loos, known for his very functional designs. But even after the end of his studies, Europe could not hold him for long: in 1923 Neutra emigrated to the United States, where he began work as a draughtsman in a New York architect's office. A year later, his wife Dione followed him, and the young couple finally moved on to Los Angeles. There Neutra worked for, among others, Frank Lloyd Wright, whose buildings fascinated the young Austrian.

In 1927 Neutra received his first major commission: a couple named Lovell entrusted the young architect with the building of a residence in the hills of Los Angeles. Neutra built a steel framework that gave an impression of lightness—until then, these were reserved for high-rise buildings—and incorporated glass surfaces. From the street entrance a wide staircase leads down to the living room and to the swimming pool in the basement. The building was nicknamed the "Health House," not however because of its inclusion of a swimming pool, but because of its health-conscious residents.

Now Neutra, barely 40, who had recently become an American citizen, raised the tempo. Over the next four decades, he created private houses at an impressive speed in his chosen home of California, supported from the 1950s by his middle son, Dion. He devoted himself to building not only villas, but also to school buildings, churches, museums, and business premises. At the same time, he was awarded honorary doctorates and exhibitions of his work in quick succession; once having passed the age of 50, he was inundated with architectural prizes and medals.

One of his best-known buildings is the vacation home begun in 1946 for Edgar J. Kaufmann. This client was already the owner of the spectacular Fallingwater House, which Frank Lloyd Wright had built a decade earlier. But for his home on the coast, near Palm Springs in California, Kaufmann had other plans. There, on a modest site of 300 square meters (and for $348,000) he created his "desert house." Neutra was inspired by the southern Californian "moon landscape": four shallow wings of the house extend into the landscape, and the walls consist mainly of glass, so that interior and exterior space merge into each other (an echo of Wright's designs). Sometimes Neutra's design is compared to a silver aircraft that has just landed on a green lawn—although the Kaufmann House, thanks to its stress on the horizontal, blends harmoniously into the barren desert landscape.

Kaufmann Desert House, Palm Springs, 1947

Kaufmann Desert House, Palm Springs, 1947

25

ALVAR AALTO

Alvar Aalto wanted to be a painter. In the end he took up his career as an architect as a compromise with his parents. But his extraordinary creativity was not to be limited just to architecture, as can be seen in some 1,000 projects, including, along with many buildings and design icons.

ALVAR AALTO

1898 Born February 3, in Kuortane, Finland

1916–21 Studies in Helsinki

1924 Marries the architect Aino Marsio

1929–32 Tuberculosis Sanatorium, Paimio, Finland

1933–34 Exhibition of his furniture in London, Milan, Helsinki, and Zurich

1935 Founds Artek

1936–54 Cellulose factory and Sunila housing project in Kotka, Finland

1937 Finnish pavilion at the Paris World Exposition

1949 Work begins on building the Technology University of Helsinki

1976 Dies May 11, in Helsinki, Finland

For his first designs as an independent architect, Aalto fell back on the language of Neo-Classicism. But soon the young Finn, described as humorous and spontaneous, turned to new ideas. The buildings of Le Corbusier and the approaches of De Stijl and the Bauhaus left their traces in Finland, too.

This stylistic transformation was not undertaken by the architect alone. For over 25 years Alvar Aalto worked together with his wife Aino, also an architect, who died in 1949. The tuberculosis sanatorium in Paimio, Finland, shows the Aaltos' altered approach around 1930: with their rows of windows, reinforced concrete and flat roofs the four different parts of the building are clearly derived from the rationalism of Le Corbusier, but they are organically joined together around the entrance area. Aalto also undertook the interior decoration of the sanatorium, and did so without exception: door handles and lamps, cupboards and chairs, are all based on his designs. Each detail was intended to contribute to the relaxation and convalescence of the patients.

It was not so much his architectural designs as his furniture projects that cemented the Finn's reputation in Europe. His furniture was so successful that from 1935 the firm of Artek, specially founded for this purpose, undertook its production—which, incidentally, it does to this day. These successes were joined by further building projects: over the next decades Aalto designed a cellulose factory together with a residential estate, as well as private houses, churches, and a university building, and the Finnish national pavilions at many international exhibitions. The Finnish architect's designs for these proved entirely individual: a curved wall, inclined forwards, adorned the Finnish exhibition pavilion at the New York World's Fair in 1939. The Technology University of Helsinki, begun by Aalto in 1949, is characterized on the outside by the use of red brick and granite. In the main hall, however, the impression is determined by concrete; moreover, the hall also fulfils its purpose when seen from the outside, as it forms the auditorium of an open-air theater. Aalto did not push himself forward as a theorist, yet his influence on later generations of architects and designers was immense. This was ensured by more than 300 assistants from all over the world who were employed by the Finn in the course of his long career.

Aalto Theater, Essen, 1983–1988

26

LOUIS I. KAHN

Public housing, but also theaters and museums, churches, factories and office buildings—Louis Kahn was clearly capable of enthusiasm for all types of building projects. The American architect and teacher searched for a long time for his own style, but his search was to be rewarded.

LOUIS I. KAHN

1901 Born February 20, in Saaremaa, Estonia (then Ösel, Russia)

1920–24
Studies architecture at the University of Pennsylvania, Philadelphia

1951–53
Yale University Art Gallery

1957 Trenton Bathhouse, Trenton, New Jersey

1957 Becomes a professor at the University of Pennsylvania

1962–75
Indian Institute of Management, Ahmedabad, India

1972 Kimbell Art Museum, Fort Worth, Texas

1969–77
Yale Center for British Art, New Haven, Connecticut

1974 Dies March 17, in New York

The Russian-born Kahn, who at the age of five had already moved to Philadelphia with his family, studied architecture at the University of Pennsylvania. Armed with his diploma, he first worked in the office of the urban planner, John Molitor, in Philadelphia, to whose commission he built exhibition buildings in the Neo-Classical style. A journey to Europe followed in 1928–1929, during which Louis Kahn also revisited his birthplace. On his return to the East Coast of the United States, Kahn, newly married to Esther Israeli, was faced with the Great Depression and worldwide economic crisis. Workless for many years, Kahn still pursued his ideas on architecture. The first opportunity to build finally presented itself in 1936. Kahn created an assembly building for the Ahavath Israel Congregation, whose unpretentiousness is impressive even from a distance: on the street side a massive block with brick cladding welcomes the visitor, with only three small windows in the stairwell breaking up the façade.

The private houses executed by Kahn over the years that followed were presented with sharp edges and entirely without decoration. The choice of materials, however, was striking: the façades were given wooden cladding, the skirtings and walls are composed of ashlar. In 1951, on his 50th birthday, the architect received his first major commission, the extension to the Yale University Art Gallery. Kahn decided in favor of a clear contrast to the historic old building and built a block with quite different façades: a totally closed brick wall closes off the building on the street side, while the back is glazed and opens into a sculpture garden.

Further large projects followed, as did honors and guest professorships. Kahn, however, often tried the patience of his clients, optimizing, altering, exploring new ideas (incidentally also in private, for he founded three families with three different women)—so that many of his designs never came into existence except on paper. One that did, however, was the research complex for medicine at Kahn's alma mater: the seven-story laboratory towers, three buildings on square ground plans, are grouped around another square, which accommodates the central amenities. Kahn extended the ensemble to the west with two six-story laboratory towers for biological research, retaining the structure of the first building: the concrete load-bearing structure is recognizable in the brick façade, while all the edges of the towers conclude in glass.

Kahn's research complex created a furor, and not only in the United States. In 1962 he gained two major commissions from Asia. In Ahmedabad, in India, he undertook the building of a commercial college. In Dhaka, he was given the responsibility for building the entire government district for the new capital. However, the first building for this project, the Parliament building, was not completed until nine years after Kahn's death.

Salk Institute for Biological Studies, La Jolla, 1959–1965

27

PHILIP JOHNSON

If there was a pop star of the architectural scene in the 20th century, it was Philip Johnson. His presence in the United States as critic, connoisseur, curator, but also architect, trendsetter and celebrity, has no equal.

PHILIP JOHNSON

1906 Born July 8, in Cleveland, Ohio

1930–36
   Becomes the founder and director of the Department of Architecture at the Museum of Modern Art in New York

1932 Curates the exhibition *The International Style: Architecture Since 1922*

1949 Glass House, his own residence, New Canaan, Connecticut

1952 Extension and sculpture garden, MoMA

1954–58
   Seagram Building, with Ludwig Mies van der Rohe

1976 Pennzoil Plaza, Houston, Texas

1979 Awarded the Pritzker Prize

1990 Crystal Cathedral, Garden Grove, California

2005 Dies January 25, in New Canaan

Philip Johnson's name is linked above all with MoMA, the New York Museum of Modern Art. As first curator of architecture from 1930 to 1936 it was Johnson who introduced the Bauhaus architects such as Ludwig Mies van der Rohe, Marcel Breuer, and Walter Gropius to the American public and helped them to world celebrity. He himself achieved fame for the exhibition The International Style organized together with Henry-Russell Hitchcock, and also for his architecture from 1922 to 1936. His collaboration with Mies van der Rohe, to whom he devoted a whole exhibition at MoMA in 1947, and his close association with the museum, were both formed during those years.

Johnson studied philosophy and history, but during his first journeys through Europe he acquired a taste for architecture. This passion continued during his time as a critic and museum worker, and so at the age of 34 he began a study course in architecture in order to create buildings of his own. The first opportunity to do so was offered to him at MoMA in 1952, when he designed the Abby Aldrich Rockefeller sculpture garden in the inner courtyard. Some ten years later he again became actively involved with the extension of the museum and the sculpture garden.

Several of his buildings have enjoyed great fame, such as the Seagram Building with the Four Seasons Restaurant in New York, built together with Ludwig Mies van der Rohe, and his own residence: the Glass House (1949) in New Canaan is a fascinating low-level building based on projects by Mies van der Rohe. It is essentially a glass box on a brick base: a steel construction with a flat roof, glass walls and a brick cylinder in the interior, which accommodates the bathroom and fireplace. This building, which lies in the middle of a park with further, very varied works by Johnson, places the living space in the heart of nature. Today it is a protected building.

The headquarters of AT&T (now the Sony Plaza high-rise) was also to be an emblematic building. This is a stone structure in a rose-gray color unusual for the 1980s, with a curved pediment whose form is historically inspired. It soon acquired the nickname of the Chippendale Building.

In addition to his own building activity, Johnson never lost sight of the architecture of others, and so, at the age of 80, he helped present contemporary avant-garde styles to the public in the exhibition *Deconstructivist Architecture*. Under this label, which is still used today, were featured the offices of Coop Himmelb(l)au, Peter Eisenman, Frank Gehry, Rem Koolhaas, Daniel Libeskind, Bernard Tschumi, and Zaha Hadid.

Rarely has an architect made use of such a wide variety of forms, something that has often been criticized in Johnson. He rose above such objections with irony and ready wit; for him, it was only a good dose of provocation that gave flavor to a debate. His burning interest in architecture and his eclectic inspiration, coupled with his social presence, made him one of the most colorful personalities in 20th-century New York.

Glass House, New Canaan, 1945–1949

28

OSCAR NIEMEYER

A better backdrop for science fiction films could hardly be imagined. Around a circular building, an elegant, weightless arc rises through the air against a blue sky; on the beach a UFO seems to have landed; and a white sphere comes to earth in the middle of Paris.

OSCAR NIEMEYER

1907 Born December 15, in Rio de Janeiro, Brazil

1934 Receives his diploma from the Escola Nacional de Belas Artes in Rio

1943 Church of San Francisco, Pampulha/Belo Horizonte

1947 Designs the headquarters of the United Nations in New York, with Le Corbusier

1955–70
Designs the building of the new capital Brasilia, with Lucio Costa

1988 Awarded the Pritzker Prize

1991 Museum of Contemporary Art the "Flying Saucer," in Niterói, Brazil

2004 Awarded the Praemium Imperiale

2007 Popular Theater of Niterói

2012 Dies December 5, in Rio de Janeiro, Brazil

These serpentine, futuristic buildings all bear the same, unmistakable hallmarks of a living myth: Oscar Niemeyer, born a hundred years ago. Since his childhood he has been drawing, at that time with his finger held up to the sky, today at his drawing board in his office near the Copacabana in Rio de Janeiro. World-famous as architect of the city of Brasilia, he has remained a supporter of revolutionary ideals—the revolution of the curve against the right angle, and the Marxist revolution for a better world. Social justice, independence of capitalism, these are the great aims to whose pursuit Niemeyer allows greater importance than to architecture: "The most important thing is life. Sometimes I think that a young man demonstrating on the street is doing more important work than I am."

When Niemeyer completed his education in the mid-1930s, he had the good luck to be able to take part straight away in an important project, working closely with Le Corbusier and learnt from him. The latter came to Brazil for three months, and between 1936 and 1943 the Health and Education Ministry came into being in Rio de Janeiro. Niemeyer's collaboration with this distinguished colleague was repeated some years later with the headquarters of the United Nations in New York.

In Brazil Niemeyer was soon offered important public commissions: after the mayor of the city, and future president of the country, Juscelino Kubitschek, had entrusted to him the design of the Pampulha district in Belo Horizonte, there followed the legendary project—the creation of a new city. Together with Lucio Costa, Niemeyer was commissioned to create out of nothing a new capital city for Brazil, Brasilia. The urban planner Costa placed on the drawing board the plan, divided by function, in which later the breathtaking concrete buildings found their places, like sculptures in an exhibition. The Catedral Metropolitana, the Congress Building with Senate and House of Representatives, and the Supreme Court in Brasilia are icons of modern building. The living accommodation in this futuristic city is controversial. Since 1987 it has been under the protection of UNESCO as a World Cultural Heritage site. Niemeyer himself believes that a visit to Brasilia could arouse different reactions, but no one could be indifferent to it. For him, this is exactly what architecture was about.

At the beginning of the new millennium he enhanced Brasilia with the National Museum, a characteristic white concrete dome with a free-floating ramp—it looks for all the world like a B-movie spaceship. In Niterói, on the side of the bay facing Rio de Janeiro, lies a whole Niemeyer promenade, or Caminho Niemeyer: a complex with a theater and a museum for contemporary art. Altogether it is to comprise 12 buildings, the greatest assembly of Niemeyer's architecture outside Brasilia.

In the course of his long career, Oscar Niemeyer has worked on more than 500 projects. His creed is beauty and surprise through free and sensual form for the enrichment of life. He has never subjected himself to the dictatorship of the right angle, but invokes the inspiring forms of nature, such as mountains and waves.

Contemporary Art Museum, Niterói, 1991–1996

Catedral Metropolitana Nossa Senhora Aparecida, Brasília, 1958–1970

29

EERO SAARINEN

Eero Saarinen said of himself that he had "grown up under the drawing board." With an architect father, Saarinen had the best possible chance of learning the trade in his early years and becoming one of America's most original designers.

EERO SAARINEN

1910 Born August 20, in Kirkkonummi, Finland

1923 His family moves to Detroit

1929–30 Studies sculpture in Paris

1934 Receives his diploma in architecture from Yale

1948 Designs the Jefferson National Expansion Memorial, St. Louis, realized in 1963 as Gateway Arch

1948–56 Builds General Motors Technical Center in Warren, Michigan

1956–63 TransWorld Airlines Terminal, John F. Kennedy International Airport, New York

1958–62 Dulles International Airport

1961 Dies September 21, in Ann Arbor, Michigan

Eero Saarinen's career is closely linked to that of his father, the architect Eliel Saarinen. In 1923 the family emigrated from Finland to the United States, and it was there that Eero Saarinen created some of the iconic images of 20th century architecture.

After completing his education, which included studying sculpture in Paris, Eero Saarinen joined his father's firm. After the latter's death in 1950 he continued to run it on his own. Eero Saarinen spent an important part of his early working years at the artists' colony Cranbrook, a park campus in Michigan dedicated to the arts. The commission to build this complex, including an academy, artists' workshops, a museum and library, had gone to his father in 1925. For several years the whole family was involved with this project. Eero concluded his study of architecture at Yale in 1934, and then traveled for two years through Europe and the Middle East. On his return, father and son founded Saarinen & Saarinen, and worked from Cranbrook until 1942.

In 1940, a team of artists working at Cranbrook with Eero Saarinen and the designer Charles Eames, won two first prizes in a competition on Organic Design for Domestic Furniture sponsored by the New York Museum of Modern Art. Over the years that followed, Eero Saarinen designed and produced furniture strongly influenced by these projects. In doing so, he also experimented with materials that contrasted strongly with the natural materials of the Arts and Crafts Movement, which had greatly influenced his youth: he now turned to fiberglass, plastic, aluminum, chrome, steel, and leather. Together with Eames, in 1945 Saarinen designed two model houses that also used new, light and industrial building materials and combinable, flexible modules.

One of Saarinen's most important projects, and at the same time one of the largest postwar commissions, was the building of the General Motors Technical Center: when it was completed after eight years, the architectural firm had quintupled in size. The complex is designed around a square artificial lake, with buildings distributed around it of various sizes in the form of boxes, with glass or porcelain façades suspended in front of them.

The complex was a stunning success, and resulted in many further commissions for Saarinen, including the premises of IBM in Rochester (1956–1958), and the technologically and formally innovative headquarters of Deere & Company in Moline, Illinois (1956–1964), with an elegant façade of pre-rusted steel and glass. In addition to these industrial buildings with their practical, clearly geometric forms, Saarinen created two structures based on circular forms on the campus of the Massachusetts Institute of Technology in Cambridge, Massachusetts: the chapel is a windowless brick cylinder, the auditorium a spherical concrete shell, more precisely a triangular section of an eighth of a sphere. The form stands on the ground at three points, with glass façades inserted between roof and floor.

Probably Saarinen's best-known building is the TransWorld Airlines (TWA) Terminal at John F. Kennedy Airport in New York. Between 1956 and 1962 a dynamic structure was created here from curved concrete shells, offering passengers beneath its sweeping roof effective routes, generously proportioned lounges and—through glass façades—a broad view of the runways. In common with Dulles International Airport in Washington, to which it is also related in other ways, it has a dynamic wave form, conveying the idea of flying.

TWA Flight Center, John F. Kennedy International Airport, New York City, 1956–1962

30

KENZŌ TANGE

The name of the architect Kenzō Tange is emblematic of Japan's new beginning after the Second World War. In Hiroshima, he built the peace memorial, an important symbol for Japan and the world. History and architecture, tradition and the future were linked in his work from this moment on.

KENZŌ TANGE

1913 Born September 4, in Imabari, Shikoku Island, Japan

1938 Receives his diploma from the University of Tokyo

1946 A member of a committee for the reconstruction of Japan, he develops plan for a new Hiroshima, and builds the Peace Memorial

1965 Awarded the RIBA (Royal Institute of British Architects) Gold Medal

1965 St. Mary's Cathedral, Tokyo

1987 Awarded the Pritzker Prize

1991 Tokyo City Hall

1996 Fuji TV Building, Tokyo

2005 Dies March 22, in Tokyo

The Hiroshima Peace Memorial Park marks the spot where the atom bomb fell. On the site of the destruction, the present-day park with its space for great numbers of visitors, stands the concrete memorial designed by Kenzo Tange, whose high arched form is related both to that of the bomb and of a traditional Japanese house. The nearby Peace Center is a long linear building in concrete on columns. This sober form takes account of its purpose; at the same time it allows us to recognize the influence of an important source of inspiration for the architect, namely that of Le Corbusier.

Apart from the work of Le Corbusier, Kenzo Tange had devoted himself intensively to questions of urban planning. The meaning of people's daily journeys to work and back, the transport routes within a city, fascinated him in particular. In 1960 he proposed a plan for the development and structuring of Tokyo, which provided for the extension across the harbor, by means of bridges and artificial islands, of this city by the sea. The solutions he sketched out for the future of the overfilled and rapidly expanding city are still being discussed today.

Although his plans for urban extension into the harbor have remained unexecuted, the cityscape of Tokyo bears Tange's unmistakable stamp. Among his most famous buildings are the two sport halls for the 1964 Olympics. Their semicircular, curved roofs with their elegant and memorable forms are suspended on steel cables, and looking at them one is easily reminded of a ship's hulk or a temple building, the shape of a comma or of a leaf. A further landmark is Tokyo's city hall. In 1991 the prefecture government moved into this building, whose two high-rise towers are centrally linked by a lower-level building. This building is a symbol of the important government tasks of the vast, present-day city, and at the same time recalls the contours of a cathedral. Another of Tokyo's sights is the headquarters of the Fuji Company, whose almost airy structure consists of bridges and struts between two huge towers. Its distinguishing mark is the sphere that sits at the highest level, which gives the building, almost entirely clad with aluminum, a playfully futuristic touch.

The destruction wrought by the Second World War brought the opportunity for young architects to replace the lost buildings with new forms. Kenzo Tange seized this chance eagerly, thus significantly contributing to the architectural image of today's Japan. While he himself emphasized the importance of Le Corbusier for his work, he combined this influence with that of Japanese architectural tradition, using his forms and materials—above all concrete—with the greatest of skill. Japan's tradition-conscious view of the future is reflected in his work.

As a teacher, Kenzō Tange was active not only in Japan, but also as a guest professor in the United States. Among his best-known students are the noted architects Fumihiko Maki, Kishō Kurokawa, and Arato Isozaki.

St. Mary's Cathedral, Tokyo, 1965

31

IEOH MING PEI

Who can think of the Louvre today and not see the glass pyramids by the Chinese-born American architect I. M. Pei? As one of President François Mitterrand's prestige projects, it was realized by means of efficient diplomacy in the face of great public resistance.

IEOH MING PEI

1917 Born Ieoh Ming Pei, April 26, in Canton, China

1940 Graduates from the Massachusetts Institute of Technology

1942 Studies with Gropius at Harvard

1946 Receives his diploma in architecture from Harvard

1955–66 I.M. Pei & Associates founded

1964–79 John F. Kennedy Library, Boston

1968–78 Extension to the National Gallery of Art, Washington D.C.

1982–90 Bank of China, Hong Kong

1983 Awarded the Pritzker Prize

1997–2003 Extension to German History Museum, Berlin

In the former royal palace, and today museum, of the Louvre, a large glass pyramid was built in the Cour Napoléon, through which the museum is entered. From here there is access to the gallery spaces, as well as the underground passages with cloakroom, shops, and cafés. It is to the rebuilding by I. M. Pei, in particular the roofing over of interior courtyards, that the museum owes a significantly greater surface area. Smaller pyramids and an inverted pyramid over the atrium of the underground shopping arcade attached to the museum complete the work. The complex of the Grand Louvre, with its pool by day and effective lighting by night, remains a popular venue.

Before this, his masterwork, Pei had already completed another important museum extension. The east wing of the National Gallery of Art in Washington was opened in 1978 after ten years' work on the project. Here an H-shaped, solid structure lies opposite the older museum. The interior rooms are on different levels and are linked by stairs and a central, triangular atrium. The museum is lit through skylights, and the atrium lies under a glass roof composed of pyramids.

The triangle and pyramid are characteristic elements in Pei's buildings. In the Bank of China in Hong Kong, completed by Pei in 1990, they are linked in a particular way. The bank headquarters is accommodated in a high-rise building of mirror glass whose entire structure is based on the triangle. Four tower units are arranged in staggered formation with pyramidal sloping roofs, creating one of the most widely visible buildings of Hong Kong. The symbolic ambition of this skyscraper was no less than to announce the economic liberalization of China.

In Germany, I. M. Pei was again commissioned to build an extension to an important museum: the German History Museum in Berlin has been considerably enlarged by the new exhibition galleries, again in a triangular building. From the old building, whose inner courtyard Pei had roofed over with steel and glass, one reaches the new museum spaces by means of an underground passage. The glass stairwell in the form of a spindle is the essential feature of the new structure, which is in direct proximity to works by an architect of the past admired by Pei, Karl Friedrich Schinkel.

Pei had come to the United States from China as a young man. He began his career as architect after the Second World War, opening his own office in New York at the age of 38. Since then, with a number of cultural institutions, but also with high-rise buildings, he has attained his declared ambition: "I carry in me the great wish to leave something behind. This has nothing to do with ego. I believe one owes it to one's own existence to leave something behind that will last."

Louvre Pyramid, Paris, 1983–1989

Extension to the National Gallery of Art, Washington D.C., 1958–1978

Bank of China Tower, Hong Kong, 1982–1990

32 GÜNTER BEHNISCH

Two impressions of the 1972 Munich Olympics have remained in the public memory: one is the terrorist attack, the other, the swinging "tent roof" over the Olympiapark. It was designed by Günther Behnisch, and is to this day inseparable from the image of Munich, an image of the triumph of the human spirit over tragedy.

GÜNTER BEHNISCH

1922 Born June 12, in Dresden, Germany

1947–51 Studies architecture at the Technische Hochschule, Stuttgart

1951–52 Works with Rolf Gutbrod

1967 Teaches at the Technische Hochschule, Darmstadt

1968 Teaches at the Technische Hochschule, Stuttgart

1968–72 Olympiapark, Munich

1980–87 Central Library of the Catholic University, Eichstätt

1990 Museum for Communication, Frankfurt

2005 Academy of Arts, Berlin

2010 Dies July 12, in Stuttgart

In 1972, when Germany invited sports people from all over the world to the Summer Olympics, the intention was to make a new German identity tangible internationally. This was also expressed by the light, open tent structure of the roofing, which Behnisch had designed and executed. In terms of engineering technology, the construction of a tent roof that was to stretch over the stadium, the sports hall and the swimming pool was a huge challenge. That this approach was successful is shown by the unbroken popularity of the Olympiapark to this day.

In 1990 Behnisch's Museum for Communication was opened in Frankfurt. The building is dominated by a glass semi-cone, by which the interior is generously supplied with daylight. Steel, glass, and wood give lightness to the museum, and the open spaces and large window areas convey the concept of "open communication." Since 2007, the museum can also be seen via the virtual world Second Life.

The Plenary Hall built in Bonn in 1992, before the move of the Bundestag to Berlin, is also intended to demonstrate openness, and to dispel distancing aura of political authority: Behnisch saw the hall as a workspace rather than a building designed to impress the public, and so it is both technologically advanced and devoid of pretentiousness of any kind. Observable from outside, it symbolizes the principle of democratic surveillance of the government's work, and the closeness of the government to the electorate. Today, after the change in capital, the hall is the centerpiece of the new World Conference Center in Bonn.

Openness is also the watchword of Behnisch's most recent Berlin building, the Academy of Arts on Pariser Platz close to the Brandenburg Gate. This was completed in 2005 after eleven years' work by Behnisch & Partner in collaboration with Werner Durth. In the interior of the glass façade of the building, the remnants of the old Academy building, in particular the historic skylit halls of the Palais Arnim-Boitzenburg, are preserved. Staircases, ramps and bridges of steel and glass dominate the interior of the new structure. Here, as he does in general, Behnisch turns away from the monumental stone architecture that he firmly rejects, particularly for ideological reasons.

With his urban structures, schools, and other public buildings, Günther Behnisch has made his mark on postwar architecture in the Federal Republic of Germany, and thus taken up a position in favor of an open and unpretentious manner of building and mentality. The library of the University of Eichstätt is among his most important works in this area. The architect has clearly distanced himself from the heavy, rigid forms that belong to the political past. This is reflected in his attitude to planning: "I feel one cannot and should not regulate everything. Otherwise what you get in the end is a sort of prescriptive architecture, which tries to control everything. No, in my houses there can be contradictions, they do not necessarily have to be right. They are open to many things, including alterations to themselves."

Olympic Park, Munich, 1968–1972

33

CESAR PELLI

The building of towers—not in Babel, but worldwide—is one of the main tasks of the firm of Pelli Clarke Pelli Architects, founded by Cesar Pelli when he was 41 years old. Today his towers stand in Europe, North America, Asia, and South America.

CESAR PELLI

1926 Born October 12, in Tucuman, Argentina

1949 Diploma in architecture from the University of Tucuman

1954–64
     Works with Eero Saarinen

1964–68
     Works with Daniel, Mann, Johnson and Mendenhall

1968–74
     Works with Gruen Associates

1976 Pacific Design Center, Los Angeles

1977 Founded Cesar Pelli & Associates

1984 Dean of the Yale University School of Architecture

1998 Petronas Towers, Kuala Lumpur, Malaysia

2004 National Museum of Art, Osaka

2008 Torre de Cristal, Madrid, Spain

2013 The Landmark, Abu Dhabi, United Arab Emirates

"Why do we build tall buildings? Very tall constructions have been built with great effort in almost all cultures all over the world. The urge to build as high as possible seems to be a basic characteristic of human culture." Of course Cesar Pelli is familiar with the Tower of Babel: "What interests me most in the Bible story is that the human desire to build as high as possible into the sky seemed to its authors to be universal." Nothing has changed to this day.

Cesar Pelli has become famous, among other things, for the most recent high-rise record before the new millennium: his twin towers in Kuala Lumpur were, at 452 meters, the tallest building in the world. Built up into the sky in forms inspired by Islam, the two skyscrapers, which are linked about halfway up by a skywalk, form a gate. Their steel and glass façades are colored gold by the sunlight. There was a thoroughly symbolic significance in the fact that these two towers brought Kuala Lumpur and Malaysia into the 21st century.

A not uncontroversial tower was created in the center of New York when, in the late 1970s, Cesar Pelli received the commission to add an extension to the famous Museum of Modern Art, MoMA. Since the opening of the museum in 1939 it had been rebuilt in several stages. Pelli enlarged the west wing and gave it a graduated glass façade. In addition, he added a tower to the museum, of which only the lower ten floors were used directly by MoMA. The exhibition areas were doubled, but the museum's strategy in improving its finances by means of the new apartments and offices was criticized, and Cesar Pelli with it.

Of course, the architect has not built only towers. His first post already brought interesting tasks along with it, for at barely 30 years of age, Cesar Pelli was working with Eero Saarinen on projects such as the TWA airport terminal in New York, and the Dulles International Airport in Washington. Both buildings are icons of the American architecture, representative of their era.

Also in Washington, D.C., Pelli's extension to the Ronald Reagan Airport was opened in 1997: a longitudinal building, highly rhythmic as a result of the roof's rounded arches, in whose interior great value is placed on the orientation and well-being of the passengers. Large window fronts offer a view of the nearby river, and light-flooded halls are adorned by artworks integrated by Pelli in the overall design.

In 2004, the National Museum of Art was opened in Osaka, a building that is the opposite of tall: here, under an eccentric sculptural formation, the exhibition galleries lie three floors below ground. This has given the museum the nickname of "the submarine." The projecting steel formation above ground accommodates the entrance area of the museum in a glass structure. This striking construction has become an important component of Osaka's cityscape and its art quarter. A specialist in tall buildings with offbeat surfaces, Pelli also demonstrates the profundity of his thought with lower-lying projects.

Petronas Towers, Kuala Lumpur, 1993–1998

34 FRANK O. GEHRY

Since 1997, when the Guggenheim Museum lifted the Spanish harbor city out of its industrial misery and transformed it into a tourist attraction, attempts have been made worldwide to copy the concept of the "specific upgrading of places through spectacular buildings by star architects." (Wikipedia)

FRANK O. GEHRY

1929 Born on February 28 in Toronto, Canada, as Ephraim Owen Goldberg

1947 Moves to California

1954 Bachelor of Architecture, USC

1982–84 California Aerospace Museum, Los Angeles

1989 Awarded the Pritzker Prize

1992 Awarded the Praemium Imperiale

1996 "Dancing House" (Ginger and Fred), Prague, Czech Republic

1997 Guggenheim Museum, Bilbao, Spain

2003 Walt Disney Concert Hall, Los Angeles

2008 Museum of Tolerance, Jerusalem, Israel

Many, for the sake of simplicity, have gone straight to the Bilbao architect himself—Frank Gehry. Gehry was by no means unknown when he was commissioned to design the museum. As early as 1989 he had been awarded the Pritzker Prize, the "Nobel Prize for Architecture." But he was an awkward customer. If you wanted conventional building forms, you would not turn to him. For Gehry, architecture is art combined with a desire to push materials and techniques to new limits.

Frank Owen Gehry was born on in Toronto, Canada, in 1929. In 1947 he moved to California, took the most varied jobs and studied architecture at the University of Southern California until 1954, and later urban development at the Harvard Graduate School of Design. It was not until 1962 that he founded his first office in Los Angeles, today called Gehry Partners LLP, with more than 175 staff. The master, however, continues to make his designs himself: models in cardboard and metalized paper, folded, crumpled, tried out and abandoned again until the shape is right and promises enough tension and effectiveness. That these little paper sculptures can be turned into buildings, into museums or concert halls, whose gravity seems to have become suspended, is thanks to a sophisticated 3-D computer program that was originally developed for the aircraft industry. With this program it is possible to calculate not only the statics of the buildings but also the material costs and production processes, and to optimize the client's specifications. Though Gehry can be a controversial architect, his buildings are kept within the agreed time frame and budget.

Gehry's style of building has continued to develop from the early 1970s to today with an unbroken record of openness to new ideas. By using unusual, supposedly "poor" materials such as plywood and corrugated iron—today they are concrete and titanium—and breaking through traditional vocabularies of form, with the introduction of a fragmented geometry of oblique and split levels, canted spaces, slits, folds, and distortions, Gehry comes across as the representative par excellence of Deconstructivism. And in fact he is one of the seven architects brought together by Philip Johnson in 1988 for the Deconstructivist Architecture exhibition at the New York Museum of Modern Art, who for the first time applied this philosophical concept to architecture. Gehry himself rejects all categorization, but with or without a label he will go down in architectural history.

Guggenheim Museum Bilbao, 1993–1997

Cleveland Clinic Lou Ruvo Center for Brain Health, Las Vegas, 2007–2010

ALDO ROSSI

ALDO ROSSI

1931   Born May 3, in Milan, Italy

1959   Receives his diploma from the Politecnico di Milano

From 1963
   Serves his apprenticeship, from 1972 at the Federal Technical College, Zurich

1970   Housing estates at Gallaratese near Milan

1971–78
   Cemetery of San Cataldo, Modena

1979   Floating Teatro del Mondo for the Venice Biennale

1990–94
   Bonnefanten Museum, Maastricht

1990   Awarded the Pritzker Prize

1997   Dies September 4, in Milan

Rossi combined universal forms and pastel colors in his characteristic compositions, whether in art or buildings. Through their use of space, both are reminiscent of the backdrops to be seen, for example, in the paintings of Giorgio de Chirico. Rossi was also a designer, and many furnishing accessories much in demand today are derived from his designs.

After completing his studies, he began his career working on an architectural magazine. All his life he made statements in writing on the theoretical problems of architecture, and as a lecturer he taught the Rationalism he practiced. As a 35-year-old he had already set out his principles in his most important book, *The Architecture of the City* published in 1966. His theoretical ambition was not a modest one: the memory of place and regional traditions are the principles on which the architectural design should be based. The forms of historic buildings are classified in types. These form the artistic forms of expression of architecture, while questions of function are important but secondary. "What I reject is merely the naïve concept of functionalism according to which functions determine form, and thus unequivocally determine urban planning and architecture." Rossi categorically rejected the famous slogan "form follows function." His view was rather that it was the continuity of the city that needed to be preserved. Thus a building, depending on its era, could alter its function, but not its historically determined image. New buildings should be adapted to the local forms of the past. The identity of a building thus arises from its time, and only a building method linked to history is able to create identity. It was Rossi's wish to supply buildings with form from the well of the collective memory—a poetic idea, whose artistic ambition must be measured by the reality of the use of his buildings.

One of his early projects is the cemetery of San Cataldo in Modena. In the middle of the geometrically designed site stands a cube, whose many little square wall openings arranged in grid form find no correspondence in the interior, and thus create a "lifeless" effect, which is precisely what was intended. This cemetery built on the principle of the square succeeds, in accordance with Rossi's theory, in expressing meaning through primary forms or types of architecture.

The repertoire of forms from which Aldo Rossi drew is related to the theater and its stage sets. For him the city was the true theater of life, and architecture the backdrop. Significantly, he built a floating theater for the 1979 Venice Biennale; his strangely timeless structure, giving the effect of stage décor, was understood as homage to an old Venetian tradition. It was recreated in 2004 on the occasion of an exhibition in Genoa.

Two years before his death, the Bonnefanten Museum in Maastricht was opened. This red-brick building is E-shaped, situated in its center is a zinc-covered, rocket-shaped tower, an eye-catcher and signature feature of the museum. The unpretentious forms in the interior, together with an abundance of daylight and wood, ensure a friendly atmosphere.

Friendly and imaginative, too, were the many drawings created in the course of time by this versatile architect and artist—and it is from them that the cities of his dreams were created.

Bonnefanten Museum, Maastricht, 1990–1994

36

RICHARD ROGERS

For more than 30 years, what is probably Richard Rogers's most famous building, in the center of Paris, has unfailingly continued to draw the crowds: the Centre Pompidou—the culture machine of the 1970s, which was designed and built together with Renzo Piano.

RICHARD ROGERS

They had the ground breaking idea of making the structure, until then always covered up, as well as functional elements of the interior, in bright colors, into the actual theme of the façade, and thus of the architecture. This concept allowed the interior spaces an unprecedented flexibility. The forecourt, today used as a social meeting point for tourists, entertainers, and passersby, had been deliberately integrated into the plans, and the concept of a cultural structure that would be easily and playfully accessible to the general public took off.

Although critics from conservative circles feared that it would be a blight on the historic center of the French capital, this monument rapidly became one of the most popular venues and attractions in Paris. Of course, this milestone of museum history was not the end of the story. Richard Rogers and his firm have created many memorable buildings, chiefly in Europe. Among these is the Millennium Dome in Greenwich, London, created for the celebration of this landmark in time, a gigantic tent structure with 12 towers rising up to the sky, like birthday candles on a cake.

Visible construction elements, mechanically playful forms, these are the characteristic components of the work of Richard Rogers. The building is turned inside out, making the functions of the architectural elements clearly recognizable.

Of the many projects of Richard Rogers, to whom, on the occasion of the 30th birthday of the building, an exhibition was dedicated in 2007 in the Centre Pompidou, the headquarters of Lloyd's in London is one of the most emblematic buildings. In the heart of the city, London's financial district, here as in the Centre Pompidou, the functional elements (such as elevators and cables) are located outside and in special tower annexes, in order to gain maximum space inside. The extension of the spaces was to remain flexible. The façade conveys the impression of a large mechanism, which matches perfectly with function of the building—the financial machine.

In recent years, Rogers has turned more and more to considerations of the durability of the building and to the conservation of the environment. Each of his projects is focused on these qualities. The building designed by Rogers in 1998 for the Welsh Assembly and occupied since 2005, for example, is very economical in its energy use when compared to traditional buildings. The appearance of the building stands for openness, democracy and participation.

A project not necessarily compatible with Rogers's political statements is One Hyde Park. In the center of London four residential towers for the super-rich have been created, whose prices, even before the completion of the building, have broken all world records. The architecture makes full use of the contemporary technological potential for the conservation of energy and materials. Made of weathered red steel and glass, this residential complex hit the headlines with its ultimate technological refinements, such as bulletproof walls and windows, private elevators, 24-hour hotel service, and the like. In the words of an estate agent, "One Hyde Park is a new residential scheme whose beauty, luxury, and prestige will place it in a class of its own."

In fact, Rogers's interest is in social improvement. He sits in the House of Lords on behalf of the Labour Party, and in his office, Rogers Stirk Harbour & Partners, value is placed on the encouragement of new talent, a commitment to charitable work, and social justice.

Lloyd's Building, London, 1978–1986

37

RICHARD MEIER

A documentary film about the architect Richard Meier proclaims him "The Magician of Light," and although he is not a magician but an architect, the title is illuminating in the truest sense of the word.

RICHARD MEIER

1934 Born October 12, in Newark, New Jersey

1952 Receives his diploma from Cornell University

1960 Works with SOM (Skidmore Owings & Merrill)

1960–63
 Works with Marcel Breuer

1963 Founds his own office

1979–85
 Museum for the Decorative Arts, Frankfurt, Germany

1984 Awarded the Pritzker Prize

1984–97
 Getty Center, Los Angeles

1987–95
 Museum for Contemporary Art, MACBA, Barcelona, Spain

1989 Awarded the RIBA (Royal Institute of British Architects) Gold Medal

1993–2000
 United States Courthouse, Islip, New York

As early as the 1960s, white villas against a blue American sky have gone into architectural history as icons of Meier's work. Clear geometrical forms, combined with intelligently arranged window areas, soon ensured his popularity as an architect.

His initial fame in the United States was due to his family houses with their characteristic white façades and light-flooded interiors. His declared favorite color is white, and only in exceptional cases does he deviate from it. It allows him, by means of skillful handling of light through generous openings in the walls, to reproduce daylight in the interior, and thus to create changing atmospheres. Meier himself says that "for me, white is the most wonderful color because within it you can see all the colors of the rainbow. For me, in fact, it is the color which in natural light, reflects and intensifies the perception of all of the shades of the rainbow, the colors which are constantly changing in nature, for the whiteness of white is never just white; it is almost always transformed by light and that which is changing; the sky, the clouds, the sun and the moon."

This is how he describes the origins of his aesthetic: "We are all affected by Le Corbusier, Frank Lloyd Wright, Alvar Aalto, and Mies van der Rohe. But no less than Bramante, Borromini, and Bernini. Architecture is a tradition, a long continuum. Whether we break with tradition or enhance it, we are still connected to that past. We evolve."

Since his beginnings, Meier has remained true to his Bauhaus-inspired style. He has brought his development and that of his firm successfully through the last 40 years, and is also represented in Europe by a large number of his projects. His unornamented, lucid buildings are particularly popular for museum architecture.

His first museum building was the Museum for the Decorative Arts in Frankfurt, built in 1985. Proportionally adapted to the existing villa, built around 1800, his three white interlinked cubes are incorporated into the park area of the Museum Mile on the Schaumainkai. Further well-known museum buildings are the Museum for Contemporary Art (Museu d'Art Contemporani) in Barcelona and the prestigious complex of the J. Paul Getty Museum near Los Angeles. On the hill lie the six buildings, linked together below ground, forming a campus that serves the museum and research institute as well as the reception of visitors. Meier's trademark white is, in this instance, exceptionally replaced by the color of the natural stone.

A self-confessed New Yorker, in 2002 Meier was able to set his seal on the city skyline in the form of two apartment towers with a view of the Hudson river—luxury living space with glamorous inhabitants, maliciously described by some as goldfish in their bowl. The two towers rise high above their neighbors, and are constructed neither of the brick typical of this part of New York, nor with an exclusively glass façade. Here glass is framed by white aluminum, placing Meier's emphasis on the urban image.

Despite the range of very different buildings he has created, his designs have characteristic features that make them recognized worldwide, notably: clear and elegant lines, the use of white, interiors flooded with light, and proportions adapted to a specific environment.

Getty Center, Los Angeles, 1991–1997

38

NORMAN FOSTER

Buildings from the Hong Kong and Shanghai Bank high-rise in Hong Kong and the Reichstag building in Berlin to the Millau viaduct in France, two and a half kilometers long, testify to Norman Foster's characteristic combination of inventive design, superb engineering, and ecological concerns.

NORMAN FOSTER

1935 Born in Manchester, England

1961 Receives a diploma from the Manchester University School of Architecture and City Planning, and a scholarship to Yale School of Architecture

1967 Founds Foster Associates, now Foster + Partners

1978 Sainsbury Centre for Visual Arts, Norwich, England

1983 Awarded the RIBA (Royal Institute of British Architects) Gold Medal

1984–92
    Carré d'Art, Nîmes, France

1994–2000
    The Great Court, British Museum, London

1999 Awarded the Pritzker Prize

2000 Millennium Bridge, London

At the age of 32, Foster, who grew up in Manchester, founded his own architectural firm, which today employs more than 1,200 staff in 22 offices worldwide. A special form of organization enables Foster to remain to the greatest possible extent informed about his many building projects.

The Sainsbury Centre for Visual Arts in Norwich, England, which apart from exhibition galleries also accommodates study and eating areas, has also contributed to his fame—a large-scale, open building, whose modular construction from ready-made parts is made visible by the supporting framework. A great deal of natural light is able to enter by day, and by night the artificial lighting gives the campus a special atmosphere. Also in the cultural area, this time in France, is the Carré d'Art in Nîmes, completed in 1993. This modern building adopts the proportions of the Roman palace opposite, and is among the museum attractions that have altered the life of a city. In London, apart from the daring structure of the Millennium Bridge and the canopy and redesign of the British Museum, it is certainly the high-rise building for the insurance company Swiss Re that has aroused the greatest public interest (and has also been a bone of contention). On the Swiss Re tower, which has been nicknamed the "Gherkin" by Londoners, and about whose construction a film has even been made, a journalist wrote: "If at least one scene of the next James Bond film is not set here, I'll eat my hat."

And Foster's buildings really are high tech, not to be outdone by anything that an inventor for an intelligence service could have devised. Even his early projects caused surprise at the economical and energy-saving way they were built, as well as the fact that they were sometimes even completed ahead of schedule.

Foster's enthusiasm and his ambition to create ever taller, larger, and more spectacular buildings have naturally also led him into the great contemporary centers of building such as Abu Dhabi, where his enterprises at the present time include projects such as the Aldar Central Market and the Masdar Development. Durability is a matter of great importance in futuristic projects, and so Masdar is an ecologically ambitions project, a green city in the middle of the desert, which is to use only half of the energy usually required. Here 40,000 individuals are to be able to live. For Foster this project represents an important symbol, intended to arouse hope of a better future—a future that he has foreshadowed with his buildings and ideas.

30 St. Mary Axe (also known as The Gherkin), London, 2001–2004

Reichstag Building (Dome), Berlin, 1992–1999

39

VON GERKAN, MARG AND PARTNERS

Berlin's Central Station was awaited with great anticipation; even the site itself was a curiosity: a viewing platform continually drew masses of curious observers. The station is among the most important to have been created in Germany in recent years.

VON GERKAN, MARG AND PARTNERS

Meinhard von Gerkan

1935 Born January 3 in Riga, Latvia

1964 Diploma rom the Technical University of Braunschweig

Volkwin Marg

1936 Born January 15 in Königsberg, East Prussia (now Kaliningrad, Russia)

1964 Diploma from the Technical University of Braunschweig

1965 The two architects found architectural partnership, Von Gerkan, Marg and Partners

1975 Tegel Airport, Berlin

1995 New Trade Fair, Leipzig

2002 Lingang New City, China

2014 Guna Villa, Latvia 2008 Arena da Amazônia, Manus, Brazil

2014 Modernization of the Estadio Santiago Bernabéu, Madrid

Admittedly its appearance does not correspond in all respects to the original design by Von Gerkan, Marg and Partners, and the media have reported on the legal disputes between the client, Deutsche Bahn, and the architect Meinhard von Gerkan, whose copyright had been infringed upon. In the meantime, not only has the dispute been settled, but also the building has been completed.

Two towers out of a steel supporting structure are linked by a barrel roof lying between them, glazed like the façades, with the outer, identically arched, platform roofs running at right angles to it. In an allusion to the tradition of railway stations with light-filled halls of steel and glass, this building was ennobled before its completion with the title "Cathedral of Mobility." A symbolic structure, in which railway tracks run crosswise from all points of the compass meet, and where the passenger changing trains has a choice of 80 shops. Above the enormous glass roof of the station, solar energy is produced in exemplary fashion.

Forty years ago, Meinhard von Gerkan and his fellow-student Volkwin Marg founded an architectural firm that today operates worldwide, with more than 300 staff. This makes it one of the largest in Germany. They have already built more than 230 buildings, and are diligently continuing to build on a large number of sites all over the world, particularly in China.

GMP became well known for building the geometrically constructed, car-friendly Tegel Airport in Berlin of 1975; airports in Stuttgart and Hamburg followed. Huge structures such as these airports, trade fair sites, stadiums, and theaters (and more recently, even whole cities) are the preferred field.

GMP's architects see themselves as artists in building. They want to combine the traditions of architecture with the possibilities of modern construction methods. Technology, art, and architecture should become one; a building method not adapted to the place, or too eccentric in form, is not their style. Volkwin Marg explains how essential it is for him to bring technology and art together into a new synthesis, the art of building: "I don't see that bridging the gulf between technology and art is a problem. This is why I am irritated by the brazenness of seemingly wise gurus who flirt with chaos and break historically evolved tectonic expressions into fractals, or blow them up to blobs based on incoherent philosophies."

GMP's buildings are technologically very ambitious, and are mostly executed within the given time frame and budget. In China, too, the firm has had a sweeping success. There, apart from many public buildings, GMP are building nothing less than an entire city. A project of superlatives—the satellite city of Lingang, near Shanghai, which is to provide living space for 800,000 individuals. "The city of Alexandria, one of the seven wonders of the world, was godfather to the design; the quality of life close to water is a reference to Hamburg." A statement such as this, between high-flying ambition and a solidly down-to-earth attitude, between idealism and a sense of reality, is characteristic of the GMP enterprise and its architectural work.

Berlin Central Station, 1996–2006

40

SOM – SKIDMORE, OWINGS & MERRILL LLP

How can one characterize Skidmore, Owings & Merrill? The firm, founded in 1936, is an anomaly—a design firm that gives technical excellence and business responsibility equal weight; one that is not centered on a single designer but rather is a collective enterprise that values collective competence.

SOM (SKIDMORE, OWINGS & MERRILL LLP)

1936 Founded by Louis Skidmore (1897–1962), Nathaniel Owings (1903–1984)

from 1939
      with John Merrill (1896–1975)

1951 Manhattan House, New York

1961 One Chase Manhattan Plaza, New York

1969 John Hancock Center, Chicago

1973 The Willis Tower, Chicago

1999 Jin Mao Tower, Shanghai

2004 Time Warner Center, New York

2009 Burj Khalifa, Dubai

2013 One World Trade Center, New York

SOM is also a business that employs nearly 1,500 architects, engineers, interior designers, and other staff, who, together, are capable of dealing with all the stages of planning projects throughout the world. Even in its beginnings, the firm focused on highly complex, large and very public commissions. Its collective nature, in which individuals remain largely anonymous, sets it apart from others. Instead of individual fame, emphasis is placed on systematic internal collaboration in design, planning, and execution. Since its founding, the firm has handled more than 10,000 projects.

The avant-garde character of SOM, accordingly, lies in its functional and formal qualities and its technological innovations, such as the early use of computers in the most varied processes, which has been systematically developed within the company (the firm developed a software for Building Information Modeling, the first of its kind, in the early 1980s). Engineering skill and a definitively rational mode of operation make SOM, among other things, the epitome of technologically impeccable skyscraper construction. But beyond this, the firm also offers expertise in the areas of urban planning and interior architecture. In its more than 70-year history, SOM has completed projects of just about every conceivable type, in countries around the world.

Among the best-known building by Skidmore, Owings & Merrill is the Sears Tower, completed in Chicago in 1974. At 463 meters, it was at that time the tallest building in the world. It followed the tradition, founded in Chicago in the 19th century, of high-rise buildings based on a steel skeleton structure, and was emblematic, as skyscrapers still are today, of prosperity, optimism, and strength. Among architectural firms in the second half of the 20th century, the SOM abbreviation was shorthand for a firm specializing in towers of this kind.

It was SOM's technical know-how that brought it the commission to build the new Freedom Tower on the site of the World Trade Center, destroyed in 2001—a project highly charged with symbolism, which in addition to great architectural challenges also needed to satisfy content-related demands. These demands are summed up as follows by SOM: "While the memorial, carved out of the earth, speaks of the past and of remembrance, Freedom Tower speaks about the future and hope as it rises into the sky." The design and building of the new tower in Manhattan are accompanied by the interest of an international public.

In Dubai, plans were made for a new "tallest skyscraper in the world," the Burj Dubai. Meanwhile, however, it was announced that another skyscraper, the Al Burj, would tower over it. In any case it is one of the tallest buildings ever built. Its structure tapers upwards in a staggered formation in order to minimize the effect of wind. The ambitious plans of the rulers of the Arab Emirates demanded that the whole world should be visible from the record heights of the Burj Dubai. What was meant were the 300 artificial islands in the bay of Dubai, which are laid out in the form of a world map. A truly Babylonian project—to reach for the sky and look down upon the world. SOM's technology makes it possible.

Burj Khalifa, Dubai, 2004–2009

41

RAFAEL MONEO

The Spanish architect Rafael Moneo is equally at home on building sites and in lecture halls. His creative career is divided between technology and texts, buildings, and books.

RAFAEL MONEO

1937 Born José Rafael Moneo Vallés, May 9, in Tudela, Spain

1961 Receives his diploma in architecture from the Escuela Tecnica Superior de Arquitectura de Madrid

1965 Founds his own firm in Madrid

1984–92 Atocha Railway Station, Madrid

1980–86 National Museum of Roman Art, Merida, Spain

1990 Chair of the Department of Architecture, Harvard University Architecture School of Design

1991–98 Museum of Modern Art and Architecture, Stockholm, Sweden

1992 Pilar and Joan Miró Foundation, Palma de Mallorca

1996 Awarded the Pritzker Prize

2003 RIBA Royal Gold Medal

The Museum of Roman Art in Merida, opened in 1986, is one of Moneo's most celebrated buildings. The city has an important Roman past, which was to be made accessible again for visitors. Situated directly next to an excavation site, the building's form and dimensions have been adapted to the historic architecture. By means of solid walls and round arches, it effectively stages an appearence recalling the Roman Empire, in which remains of buildings and archaeological objects are shown to full advantage. It is not a question of making a copy of historical buildings, but rather of the intelligent incorporation of forms from the past into a contemporary structure.

Another building created only a short time later is presented quite differently. In the middle of a hill in Palma de Mallorca, on which rapid and intensive building has been carried out, Moneo has built a veritable fortress between the former studio and private residence of the artist Joan Miró. The foundation bearing the name of the artist and his wife is accommodated in an asymmetrically serrated building, which seems to defend itself against its neighbors. Alabaster shades are applied to the windows. The sea is no longer visible from this spot on account of the dominant surrounding buildings, but the architect has made up for this by building a swimming pool on the roof. In these rooms, screened off from the noisy outside world, the beach-weary visitor can now admire the art of Joan Miró in a tranquil setting.

The presentation of art is also important at the other end of Europe: Rafael Moneo was also commissioned to build the Museum of Modern Art and Architecture in Stockholm. As a young architect he had already worked in the office of Jørn Utzon, the creator of Sydney Opera House, and was therefore able to boast some experience in Nordic countries. Composed of several building units adapted in their proportions to their surroundings, the museum stands in immediate proximity to water, on an island in the harbor. Its most striking feature are the lanterns, in the form of glass cubes, on the roof hoods, through which light enters the exhibition spaces from above.

After the success of his Stockholm museum, Moneo received the prestigious task of expanding the Prado in Madrid. He has doubled the area of the museum. Next to the venerable 18th-century art museum, the extension building is a red-brick cube standing on a granite base, with a columned façade, which fits unpretentiously, but with a character all of its own, into the urban environment. Inside, the cloister, formerly in a ruined state, rises into new life, adding a mystical element to the new structure. The newly gained spaces are primarily devoted to special exhibitions, various visitor areas and administrative offices for the museum staff.

Rafael Moneo stresses the importance of the specific location for architecture: "The shadow of anywhere is haunting our world today . . . Architecture claims the site from anywhere . . . Architecture is engendered upon it . . . The site is where architecture is. It can't be anywhere."

As a professor, Moneo teaches this principle in theoretical terms; as an architect, he proves it in practice.

Museo Nacional de Arte Romano, Mérida, 1980–1986

42

RENZO PIANO

RENZO PIANO

1937 Born September 14, in Genoa, Italy

1964 Receives his diploma in architecture from the Politecnico di Milano

1971–77 Centre Pompidou, Paris, with Richard Rogers

1988–94 Kansai International Airport, Osaka, Japan

1989 Awarded the RIBA (Royal Institute of British Architects) Gold Medal

1994–2002 Parco della Musica Auditorium, Rome

1998 Awarded the Pritzker Prize

2000–07 New York Times Building, New York

Renzo Piano says of himself that he has no style. At least not a recognizable one, not a style which makes everyone think straight away, "Ah, a building by Renzo Piano": "I don't like the idea that you have, at the earliest stages, when you start to design, to put your own stamp on a building. For example, I love working with very light elements, transparency, and natural light. So when the building's finished, you recognize those elements in some way. But I think imposing your style may be actually very limiting, because you may end by simply imposing your style, instead of understanding the need of people."

Renzo Piano researches every location before he builds on it. This creative way of going about things has made him an architect in great demand, with commissions coming from all over the world. His business, the Renzo Piano Building Workshop, with offices in Genoa and Paris, employs about a hundred staff. Piano's preoccupation with the location and the precise purpose and ambition of the building to be executed allows the creative process, from sketches by way of models to the actual building, to become a process that he loves. He explains this on the basis of his experiences in early childhood. As a small boy he often accompanied his father, a civil engineer, to building sites, and became enthusiastic about the development of a building, which appeared a magical process to him.

One of his best-known and earliest buildings is the Centre Pompidou in Paris, designed and built together with Richard Rogers. This cultural center is a favorite with the public in the middle of Paris. Piano, who lives and works quite nearby, was able to follow at close quarters the development of his cultural machine, designed—not without irony in the face of technology—like a colorful giant mechanical toy, and of the piazza in front of it.

His hobby, building his own sailing boats, allows him to carry out creative tests on new materials that may later be useful to him in his architectural projects. Technical sophistication and solid craftsmanship definitively characterize Piano's buildings. His Kansai International Airport in Osaka had just been completed when a severe earthquake in Japan caused great damage—but his wave-shaped building was unscathed.

Soon after the turn of the millennium, Piano was positively inundated with commissions in New York. He built, for example, the New York Times Building, and was entrusted with the extensions of the Whitney Museum of Art, Columbia University, and the Morgan Library. His special interest in buildings, intended to be accessible to a large public, continues unabated.

Probably one of his most exciting projects in recent years is the Jean-Marie Tjibaou Cultural Center in Nouméa, New Caledonia. Here, in allusion to the local hut structure, ten buildings of wood with steel and glass have been erected in a wildlife park as a cultural center for the Kanak culture, creating a true skyline in the middle of the island state in the Pacific.

The Tjibaou Cultural Center, Nouméa, 1991–1998

Centre Pompidou, Paris, 1971–1977

43

TADAO ANDŌ

> Ando's architecture was once compared with the Japanese tea ceremony: "Both have a deliberately created simple appearance. Both are calm, quiet, pure. Both give a feeling of expansiveness in spite of their small size. Though artificial, both are natural."

TADAO ANDŌ

1941 Born September 13, in Osaka, Japan

1951–58 Studies model building in wood with a carpenter

1969 Founds the Tadao Andō Architect & Associates in Osaka

1989 Church of Light, Ibariki, Osaka

From 1992 Buildings on Naoshima

1995 Awarded the Pritzker Prize

1997 Awarded the RIBA (Royal Institute of British Architects) Gold Medal

2001 Pulitzer Arts Foundation

2004 Chichu Art Museum, Naoshima

2006 The Langen Foundation, Neuss, Germany

2013 Asia Museum of Modern Art, Taichung City, Taiwan

This description is wonderfully accurate about the buildings created since 1969 by the former professional boxer and self-taught architect Tadao Andō. His spaces, composed of clean materials, impart an impression of nobility, and are such that visitor can, indeed must, react physically to them. The architect himself explains this with reference to the special Japanese sense of physicality, and the way in which the body reacts to specific spaces. It is such considerations that determine his approach to design. Formed from geometric elements, his minimalist designs are characterized by other pure materials such as steel, glass, wood, and his hallmark silky concrete.

The sensual (extra-sensory) element of Andō's work is visible particularly in his Church of Light in Ibariki, where the most important symbol of the Christian religion, the cross, is formed by slits in the walls through which sunlight enters a relatively dark inner space, creating a positively mystical atmosphere. It is the presence and the perception of the human being that makes the interplay of nature (sunlight) and the deliberately simple geometry into a functioning whole.

In 1992 Tadao Andō built the Japanese pavilion for the World's Fair in Seville. This consisted of a gigantic wooden building with an inward-curving façade, which was accessible by way of an arched staircase, and had a flat Teflon roof. The building resonates with clear references to Japanese architectural and craft traditions, and is at the same time very modern.

One of Andō's most impressive projects is the island of Naoshima. There he has created a center of nature and art, to which new buildings have regularly been added for more than 15 years. For example, a guesthouse and various exhibition spaces have already been built on the island, which is distant from the bustle of the city and can be reached only by boat. Here, in the middle of nature, partly resembling a natural resource, lie concrete structures in geometric forms, whose interior spaces surround the exhibited artworks with a special atmosphere. The Chichu Museum of Art (*chichu* means underground) is a concrete building for the most part buried in the earth, boasting an unusual interplay of landscape, natural light, and interior space. Lucid geometry and a highly sophisticated use of daylight give an attractive Zen atmosphere to these rooms, built to display the art of Claude Monet, Walter de Maria, and James Turrell.

In Germany, Andō has built the Langen Foundation on the Hombroich Missile Base in Neuss, which, much like the buildings on Naoshima, stands in an interesting relationship to its natural environment, with a large pool of water, earthworks, and cherry trees. Although glass walls allow a view of the outside, the exhibition rooms appear as though detached from the outside world, and form a cosmos all of their own, in which one can come closer to the artworks. Andō creates spaces for the dialogue between man, art, and nature.

His architecture is an architecture of silence: there are no noisy effects, no crashing forms, no raging demands for applause—but the positive echo is everywhere.

Church of Light, Ibaraki, 1987–1989

Chichu Art Museum, Naoshima, 2004

44

TOYO ITO

"Architecture must adapt to the diversity of society, and must reflect the fact that a simple square or cube cannot contain this diversity." It would indeed be fruitless to search for a simple square or cube in the buildings of Toyo Ito.

TOYO ITO

The curious, imaginative forms that Toyo Ito gives his buildings show the extent to which this architect has internalized this concept. For a long time it has been his declared goal to hold flowing and floating forms, ephemeres, fast in his architecture. The present, and the dynamics of big-city life, challenge Ito to responses in the form of buildings.

In 1976, in order to create a secluded space away from the bustle of Tokyo, Ito built a private house, White U, right in the center of the city. The building lies in a U-shape around a grassed inner courtyard, to which the roof gently slopes down. Light enters the inner courtyard through skylights and windows. Right next to it, several years later, Ito built his own house, which bears the poetic name Silver Hut. This hut, however, does not lie in a forest, but because of its location represents a unit largely closed off from the outside world. This one-story building consists of a roof construction of silvery reflecting steel barrel vaults, supported by reinforced concrete pillars. Above the inner courtyard is placed a removable tent roof. Thus, according to requirements, this unusual complex can be given an additional space. Interior and exterior, tradition and innovation merge naturally into each other.

One of Toyo Ito's most striking works is the Tower of Winds. Purely architecturally, this is a conversion around an exhaust air system, but visually it is an interactive installation, which reacts to the light, sound, and wind of its environment (Tokyo inner city) with its own light and sound signals. Thanks to aluminum and acrylic mirror panels, a computer-driven spectacle of colors and sounds can be experienced at night. The neon rings placed around the tower make the structure very light and almost ephemeral, further underlining the changing impulses.

As early as 1986, in an interactive tower, Ito made the interplay of technology, man, and architecture his constant theme. His preoccupation with this question was based on the nomadic status of big-city dwellers, for whom Ito developed flexible architectural units and some utopian projects. The poetic momentum of his forms and the lightness of his construction certainly originate from this attitude. His preferred materials, apart from concrete, are aluminum and every kind of perforated, punched metals, which, particularly as elements of his façades, give his buildings a kind of weightlessness.

Up to the present day, Ito has retained the ambition to do justice to the new challenges of city and environment, and offer new architectural solutions. His buildings, accordingly, are conceptually designed, and he often describes them in metaphorical terms. "To talk about architecture and explain it is difficult, for architecture inevitably has two sides. On the one hand it is an abstract model of ideas, and on the other something that exists in reality."

In the Mediatheque at Sendai there are no longer any traditional library spaces; all intervening walls are omitted in favor of an open space that is given rhythm by apparently arbitrarily grouped columns. It is Ito's declared aim to bring the physical and the virtual world into harmony in his buildings, and thus to create in his architecture spaces for our contemporary needs. In the same way, the life of the real city and the virtual cosmos are linked together. This ambition is reflected in the flowing, organic forms of the Opera House in Taichung, Taiwan.

TOD'S Omotesando Building, Tokyo, 2002–2004

45

REM KOOLHAAS

As a thinker, author, and architect, the Dutch architect Rem Koolhaas has had a great impact on contemporary architecture. Lending his voice publishing books and other writings on architectural theory.

REM KOOLHAAS

1944 Born November 17, in Rotterdam, Holland

1952–56
Lives in Jakarta, Indonesia, and from 1956 in Amsterdam

1968–72
Studies at the Architectural Association School of Architecture (AA) in London

1972–73
Studies at Cornell University, New York

1975 Founds Office for Metropolitan Architecture

2000 Awarded the Pritzker Prize

2004 Seattle Central Library

2005 Seoul National Museum of Art

2008 CCTV Center, Beijing

2013 Shenzhen Stock Exchange

2015 Garage Museum of Contemporary Art, Moscow

In *Delirious New York: A Retroactive Manifesto for Manhattan* (1978) he confronted the uncontrollable growth of cities in the age of globalization. His 1,376-page *S,M,L,XL* (1995) on the other hand gives an overview of Koolhaas's entire work up to that point, and on the other examines the connections between architecture and modern society. Incidentally, this book, whose layout, reminiscent of collages and video clips, was developed by Kohlhaas in cooperation with the Canadian graphic artist Bruce Mau, and altered the structure of architectural books worldwide.

This Dutch "prophet of a new modern architecture" was born in 1944 in Rotterdam, where today the headquarters of his Office for Metropolitan Architecture (OMA) is located. Between 1952 and 1956 he lived with his parents in Indonesia, an experience that has proved a lasting influence on him. He began his professional career as a journalist and screenwriter, before turning to architecture and studying from 1968 to 1973 at the Architectural Association in London and Cornell University in New York. Up to 1979 he was visiting fellow at the Institute for Architecture and Urban Studies in New York, which was directed by the Deconstructivist Peter Eisenman. Together with Elia and Zoe Zenghelis and Madelon Vriesendorp, in 1975 he founded OMA in London; in 1980 it was moved to Rotterdam.

During the first years there were only a few building commissions, but these created a sensation: the Netherlands Dance Theater in The Hague (1987) and the Kunsthal in Rotterdam (1992). Unexpected spatial programs, crooked levels, new forms, suspended gravity—superceding all the conventional limits. Finally, the concrete house in Bordeaux (1998) which, with a workspace that also serves as an elevator, was designed for a wheelchair user, brought him international success. With this house alone, in the judgment of the jury for the Pritzker Prize, which was awarded to Koolhaas in 2000, its creator would go down in architectural history.

The buildings that followed, always realizations of his theory of merging "bigness," technology, and progress with humanity, are no less trendsetting, such as his Netherlands Embassy in Berlin (2003), Seattle Central Library (2004), and the Casa da Música in Porto (2005). To be able to continue working on his many conceptual projects beyond architecture and urban planning, in 2002 he founded the "think tank" AMO. OMA*AMO is today directed by six partners, has more than 230 staff from 30 different countries, and runs offices in New York and Beijing. His order book is full. Hamburg, Qatar, Dubai, Beijing, and New York will soon see OMA buildings that would have been unimaginable only a few years ago.

Casa da Música, Porto, 1999–2005

China Central Television Headquarters, Beijing, 2002–2012

46

JEAN NOUVEL

Architecture students have much to learn from Jean Nouvel: how to deal with materials, light and shade, transparency and the illusion of dematerialization, the richness of metaphors, the unexpectedly new and different, the playful and the serious, elegance and the grand gesture—all expressed in built architecture.

JEAN NOUVEL

1945   Born August 12, in Fumel, Lot-et-Garonne, France

1966–72
       Accepted as best applicant at the École Nationale Supérieure des Beaux-Arts in Paris; 1972, receives diploma in architecture

1967–70
       Assistant to Claude Parent and Paul Virilio

1995   Becomes an honorary member of the Royal Institute of British Architects, London

2000   Golden Lion of the Venice Biennale

2007   Paris Concert Hall

2009   Serpentine Gallery Pavilion, London

2010   One New Change, London

2012   Duo Towers, Paris

2014   One Central Park, Sydney

Nouvel's first building to attract attention is the Institut du Monde Arabe, with which he achieved his international breakthrough. It was one of the Grands Projets of François Mitterrand, who helped Paris to achieve new splendour in the 1980s through symbolic major projects. The Institut du Monde Arabe received the Equerre d'Argent for the best French building in the year of its completion, 1987. There followed one masterpiece after another, such as the rebuilding of the Opéra Nouvel (Nouvel Opera House) in Lyon, whose new glass barrel roof merges with the 19th-century substructure into a harmonious "total work of art" (for this too, Nouvel received an Equerre d'Argent in 1993); the main body of the Fondation Cartier in Paris, apparently dematerialized between two reflecting glass walls; the 1995 Galeries Lafayette store in Berlin; and, in 2000, the Culture and Convention Center Lucerne, which with its strongly protruding roof makes an unprecedented architectural statement and at the same time reflects the lake and the surrounding mountain world. The Torre Agbar, Barcelona's new landmark, towers up from the ocean of houses like a monolith, its colors constantly changing, while the Musée du Quai Branly in Paris, which opened in 2006 and is dedicated to the art of Africa, Oceania, and Asia, with its apparently arbitrary juxtaposition of the most diverse structures, speaks a whole new architectural language.

Born in 1945 in the small village of Fumel in southwest France, Jean Nouvel at first wanted to study painting, but then signed up for architecture and in 1970, while still a student, founded his first architectural office. Brought up in the political climate of the 1960s, he also became committed to the social role and political responsibility of architecture. In 1976 be became a cofounder of the architectural movement Mars, and a year later of the Syndicat de l'architecture, which is still active today. In 1978 he founded the Architectural Biennale in the context of the Paris Biennale.

The Ateliers Jean Nouvel, founded in 1994, today employ more than 150 staff from 25 countries, where not only architects, but also urban planners, landscape architects, model builders, graphic artists, industrial designers, and interior designers work together. Jean Nouvel Design reflects the master's enthusiasm for product design. In the Ateliers, work is in progress on more than 40 projects to be realized worldwide in the next few years.

Torre Agbar, Barcelona, 1999–2005

47

DANIEL LIBESKIND

His first building struck the architectural landscape like a bolt of lightning. Usually the beginning of an architect's career is marked by smaller commissions. Libeskind's first work, however, was Berlin's Jewish Museum, which made him world-famous in an instant.

DANIEL LIBESKIND

1946 Born May 12, in Lodz, Poland

1957 Emigrates with his family to Israel, and studies music there

1965–70 Becomes an American citizen, and starts a course of study in architecture at the Cooper Union of the Advancement of Science and Art, New York

1971–72 Postgraduate study of architectural theory and history at the School of Comparative Studies, Essex, England

1997 Awarded an honorary doctorate by the Humboldt University, Berlin

1999 Jewish Museum Berlin

2003 World Trade Center Masterplan

2011 Reflections at Keppel Bay, Singapore

2015 Vanke Pavilion, Milan

Not, of course, on account of the sheer size of the museum, but because of its unusual structure and power of expression. The metaphor of lightning is apt here not only in a figurative sense; it is also at the basis of the ground plan, which Libeskind has significantly conceived as a distorted Star of David. So-called "voids," empty spaces extending over five floors in the interior of the building, symbolize the absence of the Jewish population of Berlin. Slanting window slits cut like knife slashes into the outer skin of the building.

These examples demonstrate Libeskind's understanding of architecture: for him architecture is a language—full of metaphors, allusions, and historical references to the place for which it is intended. His plans and sketches are scattered with explanations and addenda. Philosophy, literature, history, music: all disciplines flow into his Deconstructivist designs, which brings him on the one hand an enthusiastic band of followers and on the other the criticism that his architecture is overloaded with meaning.

This intellectual, always black-clad, gentle, and friendly outsider was born 1946, the son of Jewish Holocaust survivors, in Lodz, Poland. His family emigrated to Israel in 1957 and settled in the USA in 1960. In 1965 Libeskind became an American citizen. Before turning to architecture, he studied music in Israel and at first practiced as a professional musician. Between 1965 and 1970 he studied at the Cooper Union School of Architecture, New York, and between 1970 and 1971 studied architectural history and theory as a postgraduate student at the University of Essex in England. There followed years of teaching at various English universities and in the United States. For the building of the Jewish Museum, he moved to Berlin with his family in 1989. He attracted further attention with various follow-up commissions such as the Danish Jewish Museum in Copenhagen, the spectacular Imperial War Museum in Manchester and a private gallery in Majorca. He was heaped with awards and honorary doctorates. But what finally catapulted him into public attention worldwide was the first prize in the 2002 competition for the Ground Zero master plan in New York.

With this remarkable design, Libeskind remained true to his principle of architecture parlante. The buildings' names alone speak volumes—Memory Foundations, Freedom Tower—as do the symbolism of numbers (the Freedom Tower was to be 1,776 feet high, a reference to the year of the Declaration of Independence) and the formal and visual references to the Statue of Liberty. But real life spoke a different language. The site owners and developers found the design too extravagant and too expensive. What remained of the dream of the Freedom Tower was merely the height of 1,776 feet (541.3 meters), after another firm, SOM, had been entrusted with executing the plans. Of the overall plan, only the Memory Foundations remain on the project list of Studio Daniel Libeskind (SDL), which moved to New York in 2003 and employs 70 staff there. But in the wake of the Ground Zero debate, SDL is booming. Further branches of the firm have opened in Zurich, Milan, San Francisco, Denver, Toronto and wherever new Libeskind buildings are being created; orders have come in since then from all over the world.

Denver Art Museum (Hamilton Building), 2003–2006

Jewish Museum Berlin, 1989–1999

48

STEVEN HOLL

Steven Holl conceived the St. Ignatius Chapel on Seattle University's campus is based on "seven bottles of light in a stone box," whereby each color of light, in the different sections of space in the building, are arranged according to liturgical symbolism, and created by colored windows in the interior.

STEVEN HOLL

The forms filled with light by Steven Holl are of the most varied shapes. What is common to his buildings as a special feature, however, is his use of natural or artificial light, and its skilful continuation into the interior of the architectural structure.

On completing his studies in Washington and Rome in 1976, Steven Holl opened an office in New York, which remains today the base for his activities. A further office has been added in Beijing. At the beginning of his career he published the magazine *Pamphlet Architecture*, and his preoccupation with architectural theory has continued for almost 30 years in his work as a professor at Columbia University in New York.

His creative approach to his designs is often conceptual and driven by philosophical considerations. Often he sums up his concept in a few words noted on his artistic sketches. For Holl, inspiration is always closely connected with the prospective site of the intended building.

In the case of the Bloch Building of the Nelson-Atkins Museum of Art in Kansas City, Missouri, opened in 2007, it could have been the inscription of the façade of the existing museum from the 1930s, with its imposing columned frontage, that led him to his concept: "The soul has greater need of the ideal than of the real."

Here, on the basis of the opposing pair, stone and feather, Steven Holl developed a series of formal demands on the extension building for which he had been commissioned. The great majority of the new exhibition spaces are located underground. As complementary contrasts to the old museum and its surrounding park, five irregularly formed building structures are visible above ground level, which are linked together underground. The lenses (as the architect calls the upper parts of the extension building) are composed entirely of special frosted glass. This matches the color of the sky by day, and conveys the light to illuminate the dynamically designed interior spaces. At night, the glass boxes, now appearing to be floating, are lit up and form surrealistic-looking sources of light for the park and the sculpture garden.

Steven Holl was able to realize a variant of this play with light faculty in the Department of Philosophy at the City University of New York: here it is a question of an interior rebuilding, whose concept is derived from Holl's interest in phenomenology and the theories of Ludwig Wittgenstein. Unusual reflections of light are created in the newly designed stairwell—as an inspiration for the students who pass through?

Steven Holl's largest undertaking to date is a city within a city, an impressive residential development in Beijing. Linked Hybrid, as it it known, on account of its multifarious uses, with residential areas, shops, leisure centers, and offices. Eight asymmetrically positioned towers are linked together by bridges. As with many of Holl's projects, great value is placed on ecology. The complex is geothermally air-conditioned. One comment stated that the complex was like a 21st-century version of the Forbidden City. Holl's city, however, will be very accessible.

Bloch Building for the Nelson-Atkins Museum of Art, Kansas City, 1999-2007

49

ZAHA HADID

If her brothers had had their way, she would have become the first female Iraqi astronaut. Instead Zaha Hadid was the first woman to have received a Pritzker Prize (in 2004) and to be among the world stars of architecture. That should satisfy even the most ambitious of brothers.

ZAHA HADID

1950   Born October 31, in Baghdad, Iraq

1972–77
        Studies at the Architectural Association School of Architecture in London

1978–80
        Works as a partner in the Office for Metropolitan Architecture with Rem Koolhaas and Elia Zenghelis, London

1980   Founds her own office

1988   Takes part in the exhibition *Deconstructivist Architecture* at MoMA, New York

2004   Awarded the Pritzker Prize

2006   Retrospective at the Guggenheim Museum, New York

2009   Burnham Pavilion, Chicago

2011   BMW Central Building, Leipzig

2016   Dies March 31, in Miami

But success came only after years of consistent hard work—and until a client had the courage to translate Hadid's architectural visions into reality. For however much her abstract drawings were admired and her competition designs were honored with prizes, they were ahead of their time and considered as simply impractical.

Single-minded belief in progress had been Zaha Hadid's heritage from birth. The mood in Iraq at the time was marked by optimism. Born in Baghdad in 1950, she received an excellent education, made possible by her parents, and crowned, between 1972 and 1977, by a course of study at the Architectural Association in London. Her teachers, Rem Koolhaas and Elia Zenghelis, of whose Office for Metropolitan Architecture she was a member between 1978 and 1980, were ideal patrons and encouraged her in the further development of her spatial concepts.

Influenced by Russian Constructivism and on the lookout for new presentation media beyond simple engineering drawings, Hadid first adopted painting as a medium of expression. In order to depict adequately our complex, postmodern age with its ever changing dynamics and new social structures, spatiality had to be newly defined: space itself was distorted and displaced, layered and overlaid, so that a new space continuum could be created. Hadid's early sketches look as though they had been drawn on a computer, long before such programs came on the market.

In 1980 Hadid founded her own architectural office in London. During the following decade, however, her desk was heaped not with building commissions, but with teaching appointments. The lecture halls of the most renowned architectural schools were full to bursting when she spoke on her concepts. She won competitions. Her 1983 design for the restaurant on Hong Kong's Victoria Peak has since become iconic, at least since 1988 when it was exhibited in the celebrated Deconstructivism exhibition at the Museum of Modern Art in New York. But it has never been built.

The first of Hadid's structures in real concrete, steel, and glass came into being in 1993, with the fire station of the Vitra furniture company in Weil am Rhein: an architectural sensation. Her next competition designs, including the Cardiff Bay Opera House (first prize in 1994), again remained unrealized. It was only the elegant Bergisel ski-jump in Innsbruck (2002) and the Rosenthal Center for Contemporary Art in Cincinnati, Ohio, (2003) that finally brought the breakthrough. Since then, cultural centers, industrial headquarters, and sports facilities have emanated, and are still emanating worldwide, from the laboratory of this energetic woman. Her architecture is probably best suited to the 21st century.

Phaeno Science Center, Wolfsburg, 2000–2005

Heydar Aliyev Center, Baku, 2007–2012

50

HERZOG & DE MEURON

None of their buildings is like any other. The designs from the studio of the two Swiss architects Jacques Herzog and Pierre de Meuron are all of the very highest quality—each individual building is a tailor-made one-off.

HERZOG & DE MEURON

1950   Jacques Herzog and Pierre de Meuron born in Basel, Switzerland

1970–75   They study architecture at the Federal Institute of Technology (ETH), Zurich

1978   Found a joint architectural practice in Basel

2001   Awarded the Pritzker Prize

2002   Found the ETH Studio, Basel

2007   Awarded the RIBA (Royal Institute of British Architects) Gold Medal

2007   Praemium Imperiale of the Japan Art Association

2011   Serpentine Gallery Pavilion, with Ai Weiwei, Kensington Gardens, London

2013   Meret Oppenheim Tower, Basel

The characteristic quality of their architecture lies not in a recognizable, repeating vocabulary of forms, but on another level. It is its constant ability to surprise and amaze, its innovative use of materials and new developments in construction technique. It is its impressive quality of design, its Swiss precision, and at the same time its total artistic freedom; not only do the buildings have the effect of works of art, but many also come into being in close cooperation with artists such as Rémy Zaugg, Thomas Ruff, Rosemarie Trockel, Michael Craig-Martin, and Ai Weiwei. That the function of a building cannot be read from its outer form is another trait of the architecture of Herzog and de Meuron. At the same time, however, all their buildings are outstandingly appropriate to their purpose, whether they are art galleries, sports stadiums, or administrative buildings. And they are clearly conceived solely for the place where they stand. Not only the topography, but also the constraints and needs of the location are seen by Herzog and de Meuron as a challenge and an opportunity to find new constructive and aesthetic solutions. However much their most recent works oppose our visual habits, they arouse thoroughly positive emotions. More than this, they creep into the hearts of their users, often even before they are completed, and become the trademark of a firm, the symbol of a city, the pride of a nation.

The architectural duo have for a long time been supported by seven partners and more than 250 staff, distributed worldwide in offices in Barcelona, Peking, Munich, London, and San Francisco. But the headquarters of the firm is in Basel, where both Jacques Herzog and Pierre de Meuron were born (on April 19 and May 8, 1950, respectively). What is remarkable is that the two have not only worked together since they both studied architecture at the Federal Institute of Technology (ETH) in Zurich (1970–1975), but have actually been friends since their childhood days, even if their sandcastles and Lego houses of those days did not yet hint at their later career, and both came to architecture only by a roundabout route. After completing their studies, both continued for three years as assistants at ETH, and in 1978 they founded their own office in Basel, which grew slowly but steadily in importance.

Apart from building commissions, they also accepted teaching appointments: at Harvard University (from 1993) and at the ETH in Zurich (from 1999) up to the present day. Although they were already long known beyond the borders of Switzerland, their rebuilding of a former power station in London as a museum space for the Tate Modern gallery in 2000 brought them their international breakthrough. And it was undoubtedly their brilliant rededication of a gigantic industrial building that led to the Pritzker Prize in 2001, and to worldwide major commissions such as the extension to the Walker Art Center in Minneapolis (2005), the Allianz Arena in Munich (2005), the Hamburg Elbphilharmonie concert hall (2008), and the Olympic stadium in Beijing (2008). The National Stadium, known as the "Bird's Nest" on account of its outer skin of steel "twigs," was hailed by *Time* magazine as early as a year before its completion as one of ten architectural masterpieces of 2007.

Elbphilharmonie, Hamburg, 2003–2016

National Stadium, Beijing, 2003–2008

153

GLOSSARY

ARCHITECTURAL TREATISES

The oldest surviving architectural treatise is that of the Roman architect, engineer, and writer Vitruvius, *De architectura* (c. 33–14 BC). Preserved from the Middle Ages are the writings of the French cathedral architect and Abbot of Saint-Denis, which deal primarily with the symbolic meaning of an ecclesiastical building. Vitruvius's text was then taken up again in the Renaissance, above all by the architectural theorist Leon Battista Alberti in his treatise *De re aedificatoria*, first published in full in 1485 as *On the Art of Building in Ten Books*. Following Alberti, many Renaissance architects, such as Filarete, Serlio, and Palladio, also left writings. Architects of later centuries added their contributions, until the flow of treatises finally declined in the 19th century, when they were often on the revival of much older styles, only to be revived in the 20th century.

ART NOUVEAU

Around the mid-19th century, the Arts and Crafts Movement developed in Britain: its aim was to revive artistic craftwork on the model of medieval craft traditions. Resistance to industrialization and mass production soon grew, with designers returning to earlier styles, notable those of the Middle Ages and the Renaissance. Throughout Europe and North America, architects, painters, designers and sculptors, as well as cabinetmakers, glass artists, potters, and jewelers were reviving the traditions of past centuries. Rejecting the straight lines and strict proportions of Neo-Classicism, they employed curved lines and richly decorative ornamentation that alluded to natural and vegetal forms. This movement was known as Art Nouveau in France and elsewhere, Jugendstil in Germany, and Modernisme in Spain.

BAROQUE

The Baroque was the age of opulence, spectacle, and impressive display. With their major commissions, influential rulers, both religious and secular, determined the character of the rich creative products of 17th- and 18th-century art. The declared aim, above all in Catholic Europe, was nothing less than the creation of a "total work of art": all artistic forms of expression were meant to work together, architecture, sculpture and painting as well as literature and gardening, fashion and music. The final form of the Baroque style, lighter in style and mood, is known as Rococo.

DE STIJL

The painter Theo van Doesburg created the Dutch visual arts magazine *De Stijl* in 1917, and it continued to appear until 1932. It was around this magazine that a celebrated group of artists and designers formed. As well as Van Doesburg, Piet Mondrian was a member from the beginning, and many other painters, architects, and sculptors came together in De Stijl. Whatever their métier, they demanded an art that went beyond the imitation of nature: turning against the depiction of natural forms, they resorted to simple geometrical forms and clarity of color. Their works were largely characterized by horizontal and vertical elements, by the colors red, blue, and yellow, and by the neutral tones black, white, and gray. The movement influenced architecture mainly through Rietveld's Schröder House.

HIGH-RISE BUILDINGS

The concept of the skyscraper became established in the last third of the 19th century in Chicago. Originally called "cloudscrapers," they were buildings whose height demanded the incorporation of elevators, a new technology. Such buildings were made possible by the use of a steel framework: it is this rather than the walls that bear the weight of the building, which can now be filled with glass. The first skyscrapers were primarily office buildings; residential high-rise buildings were not created until the 1930s. The second great showplace of high-rise architecture was New York, where in the early 1930s the Chrysler and the Empire State Building competed for the title of tallest building in the world. Since then, this competition has become a never-ending one. At present the Burj Dubai in Dubai, which is intended to reach 700 meters high, is in first place.

INTERNATIONAL STYLE

With his clear, purist language of forms, Mies van der Rohe is considered the founder of the International Style, which attracted devotees particularly in the 1930s and 1940s, above all in Europe and the USA. "Fitness for purpose" was at the overriding aim of the adherents of this movement. Buildings in this style consist of simple basic forms, often arranged asymmetrically, their white rendering interrupted only by horizontal window strips. Light and mass determine the impression. In 1932 Philip C. Johnson and Henry-Russell Hitchcock dedicated an exhibition to this style, The International Style: Architecture Since 1922, thus formalizing the concept of the International Style.

NEO-CLASSICISM

Since the Renaissance it has been impossible to exclude the classical buildings of Rome from the architectural canon. In the 1760s the French revolutionaries discovered Greek antiquity as a model. In the decades that followed, many architects worldwide once again followed the architectural forms of Greek and Roman antiquity. This phenomenon became known as Neo-Classicism. During the 19th century in Europe and North America, it was not only classical but also other older styles that were adopted, from Oriental building traditions to the Romanesque and, above all, the Gothic styles, a trend known as revivalism.

PALLADIANISM

Palladio's buildings and architectural writings were to remain highly influential throughout the centuries. In the 17th century the celebrated architect Inigo Jones imported the teachings of his Italian role model into England, and in the Netherlands, Scandinavia, and Germany many architects were also inspired by Palladio's designs. The wave of Palladianism even swept over North American shores; in the late 18th century, a number of private houses and public buildings in the United States were built on the model of his country villas. The American president Thomas Jefferson, notably, planned his countryseat, Monticello in Virginia, closely following the style of Palladio's Rotonda (see page 37).

RENAISSANCE

The Italian art historian Giorgio Vasari coined the concept of the "rebirth," the *rinascimento*, of the arts. In his view, after the gloomy Middle Ages, painting could flourish once again. Later the term Renaissance was also applied to sculpture, architecture, philosophy, and literature. Characteristics of the culture of this era include references to works of classical antiquity, a debate on perspective, and a new understanding of man as the crown of creation. The Renaissance first flourished in the wealthy Florence of the 15th century, but after the turn of the century Rome became its new center. The popes above all were great patrons of the arts, for the harmony seen in buildings, sculptures, and paintings was considered a reflection of divine order. The arts were also, importantly, a vivid expression of the Church's power and authority.

THE ARCHITECT AS ARTIST

"Remember that no other memory remains of us than the walls, which after hundreds and thousands of years still bear witness to him who was their author." The historian Giorgio Vasari cites these words of the architect Filippo Brunelleschi, who was very anxious to be regarded not as a simple craftsman, but as an artist. Architects, after all, drew on the traditions of the liberal arts, above all those of geometry and arithmetic, so there was no reason not to see them as artists. A number of the noted architects of the Renaissance fought for a revaluation of their profession, and with success: unlike that of painters and sculptors, the status of architects as artists in their own right was already recognized as early as the 15th century.

PORTRAIT ILLUSTRATIONS

01 FILIPPO BRUNELLESCHI
Andrea di Lazzaro (Buggiano) Cavalcanti, Bust, date unknown

02 LEON BATTISTA ALBERTI
Leon Battista Alberti, Self-Portrait, c. 1436

03 DONATO BRAMANTE
Portrait in a painting, date unknown

04 MICHELANGELO
Jacopino del Conte, Portrait of Michelangelo, c. 1535

05 ANDREA PALLADIO
Friedrich Wilhelm Meyer, Portrait of Andrea Palladio, c. 1810

06 GIAN LORENZO BERNINI
Self-Portrait, 1665

07 CHRISTOPHER WREN
Engraving based on a painting by Godfrey Kneller (from 1711), 1801

08 JOHANN BALTHASAR NEUMANN
Marcus Friedrich Kleinert, Portrait of Balthasar Neumann, 1727

09 CLAUDE-NICOLAS LEDOUX
Martin Drolling, Portrait of Claude-Nicholas Ledoux, 1790

10 THOMAS JEFFERSON
Engraving based on a painting by Gilbert Stuart (from 1811), date unknown

11 KARL FRIEDRICH SCHINKEL
Carl Friedrich Ludwig Schmid, Portrait of Karl Friedrich Schinkel, 1832

12 GOTTFRIED SEMPER
Photograph, date unknown

13 OTTO WAGNER
Photograph, c. 1910

14 DANIEL BURNHAM
Photograph, date unknown

15 ANTONI GAUDÍ
Photograph, c. 1882

16 LOUIS SULLIVAN
Photograph, c. 1895

17 VICTOR HORTA
Portrait of Victor Horta, published in *La Belgique d'aujourd'hui*, 1908

18 FRANK LLOYD WRIGHT
Photograph, date unknown

19 AUGUSTE PERRET
Photograph, date unknown

20 WALTER GROPIUS
Photograph, 1920

21 LUDWIG MIES VAN DER ROHE
Photograph, 1933

22 LE CORBUSIER
Photograph, 1950

23 GERRIT RIETVELD
Photograph, date unknown

24 RICHARD NEUTRA
Gert Schütz, Richard Neutra in Berlin, 1959
© akg-images/Gert Schütz

25 ALVAR AALTO
Photograph, date unknown

26 LOUIS I. KAHN
Fred W. McDarrah, Portrait from Louis I. Kahn, 1973

27 PHILIP JOHNSON
Ted Tha, Philip Johnson at work, 1979

28 OSCAR NIEMEYER
Sergio del Grande, Oscar Niemeyer infront of Mondadori Palace, 1976
© Mondadori Portfolio via Getty Images

29 EERO SAARINEN
Photograph, date unknown

30 KENZO TANGE
Photograph, date unknown

31 IEOH MING PEI
Photograph, date unknown

32 GÜNTER BEHNISCH
Photograph, date unknown

33 CESAR PELLI
Photograph, 2007
© Photo by Getty Images for Red Building

34 FRANK O. GEHRY
Todd Eberle, Portait of Frank O. Gehry, date unknown

35 ALDO ROSSI
Photograph, 1993

36 RICHARD ROGERS
Bruni Meya, Portrait of Richard Rogers, 1998
© akg images/Bruni Mea

37 RICHARD MEIER
Irving Penn, Portrait of Richard Meier, date unknown

38 NORMAN FOSTER
Andrew Ward, Portrait of Norman Foster, date unknown

39 GERKAN, MARG UND PARTNER
Wilfried Dechau, Portrait of Meinhard von Gerkan, 2003; Wilfried Dechau, Portrait of Volkwin Marg, 2009

40 SOM
Photographs, dates unknown

41 RAFAEL MONEO
Photograph, date unknown

42 RENZO PIANO
Gianni Berengo Gardin, Portrait of Renzo Piano, date unknown

43 TADAO ANDŌ
David Woo, Portrait of Tadao Andō, date unknown

44 TOYO ITO
Alessandra Benedetti, Portrait of Toyo Ito, 2017
© Corbis/Corbis via Getty Images

45 REM KOOLHAAS
Photograph, date unknown

46 JEAN NOUVEL
Photograph, date unknown

47 DANIEL LIBESKIND
Franco Origlia, Portrait of Daniel Libeskind, 2016
© Getty Images

48 STEVEN HOLL
Mark Heithoff, Portrait of Steven Holl, date unknown

49 ZAHA HADID
Steve Double, Portrait of Zaha Hadid, date unknown

50 HERZOG & DE MEURON
Todd Eberle, Portrait of Jacques Herzog and Pierre de Meuron, date unknown

The illustrations in this production have been kindly provided by institutions, and archives mentioned in the captions, or taken of the following:

akg-images: Manuel Cohen: p. 9, Cover, Rabatti – Domingie: p. 11, Schütze/Rodemann: pp. 15, 52, 72, Erich Lessing: p. 37, Bruni Mea: p. 110, Jürgen Raible: p. 51, Gert Schütze: p. 78; Archives nationales/Institut français d'architecture, Fond Perret: p. 62; Achim Bednorz, Cologne: pp. 13, 27; ARTUR: Hans H. Münchhalfen: p. 33, Karin Heßmann: p. 74, Dieter Leistner: p. 83, Arndt Oehmichen: p. 97, Christian Richters: p. 135, Roland Halbe: p. 141; Iwan Baan: pp. 152/153; Bauhaus Archive Berlin: p. 68; Behnisch & Partner, courtesy Behnisch Architekten: p. 100; Bilderberg, Hamburg: pp. 19, 47; Marcus Bredt: p. 119; Burg/ Schuh BFF, Palladium Fotodesign, Cologne/ Berlin: p. 109; Lluís Casals: p. 123; Steve Double: p. 146; Todd Eberle: pp. 104, 150; Hans Engels: pp. 70/71; Gianni Berengo Gardin: p. 124; John Gollings: p. 125; courtesy Mark Heithoff: p. 144; Werner Huthmacher: p. 147; Getty Images: p. 86, Darrell Godliman: pp. 24/25, Hedrich Blessing Collection/Chicago History Museum: p. 53, Sergio del Grande\Mondadori Portfolio: p. 88, For Red Building p. 102, Alessandra Benedetti - Corbis/Corbis: p. 132; Franco Origlia: p. 140, Sean Gallup: p. 151; Rainer Kiedrowski: p. 101; IFA Bilder-team, Munich, Siebig: p. 111; laif: pp. 61, 63, 66/67, 73, 77, 79, 85, 105, 113; Alexander Langkals, Landshut: p.9, Frontispiece; Heiner Leiska: p. 118; LOOK: p. 35; Mitsuo Matsuoka: p. 129; mauritius images: Arcaid Images/ Alamy: p. 56, age fotostock/Kino/VWPics: pp. 90/91, STOCK4B-RF: p. 101, Steve Vidler: p.103, robertharding/ Michael DeFreitas: p. 106/107, Hermis.fr./ GARDEL Bertrand/hermis. fr: p. 121, Axiom Photographic/Dosfotos: p. 139; Norman McGrath: p. 87; Florian Monheim / Bildarchiv Monheim GmbH: S.29–31 ; NACASA & Partners, courtesy of TOD's: p. 133; Werner Neumeister: p. 65; John Nye, Hong Kong: p. 99; Postsparkasse Wien Bibliothek: p. 43; Andy Ryan: p. 145; Giovanni Simeone: pp. 20/21; The Solomon R. Guggenheim Museum, New York, Fotograf: David Heald © SRGF, New York: p. 60, cover; Tim Street-Porter/Esto: p. 80; Ezra Stoller/Esto: pp. 69, 98; Studio Daniel Libeskind: pp. 141–143; Tadao Ando Architects and Associates: pp. 130/131; Andrew Ward: p. 114; Nigel Young/Foster + Partners: pp. 114/115

Cover: Frank Lloyd Wright, Solomon R. Guggenheim Museum, New York City, see page 60; Filippo Brunelleschi, Cathedral of Santa Maria del Fiore, Florence, see page 9

Frontispiece: Leon Battista Alberti, Santa Maria Novella (detail), Florence, see page 62

Texts by Isabel Kuhl: pp. 8, 10, 12, 14, 18, 22, 26, 28, 32, 36, 40, 42, 46, 48, 52, 54, 58, 62, 64, 68, 72, 76, 78, 82, 84
Texts by Kristina Lowis: pp. 88, 87, 92, 94, 96, 102, 108, 110, 113, 114, 118, 120, 122, 124, 132, 128, 144
Texts by Sabine Thiel-Siling: pp. 104, 134, 138, 140, 148, 150

© Prestel Verlag, Munich · London · New York, 2017
A member of Verlagsgruppe Random House GmbH, Neumarkter Strasse 28 · 81673 Munich

In respect to links in the book, Verlagsgruppe Random House expressly notes that no illegal content was discernible on the linked sites at the time the links were created. The Publisher has no influence at all over the current and future design, content or authorship of the linked sites. For this reason Verlagsgruppe Random House expressly disassociates itself from all content on linked sites that has been altered since the link was created and assumes no liability for such content.

Prestel Publishing Ltd.
14-17 Wells Street
London W1T 3PD

Prestel Publishing
900 Broadway, Suite 603
New York, NY 10003

Library of Congress Control Number: 2017931925

Editorial direction: Claudia Stäuble, Adeline Henzschel (of the updated edition)
Translation: Christine Shuttleworth
Copyediting: Chris Murray, Leina González Braid (of the updated edition)
Picture editing: Veronika Wilhelm, Adeline Henzschel (of the updated edition)
Cover design: Sofarobotnik
Design: normal industries, Munich
Typesetting: Wolfram Söll
Production management: Corinna Pickart
Separations: Reproline Mediateam, Munich
Printing and binding: Druckerei Uhl, Radolfzell

Paper: PrimaSet
Verlagsgruppe Random House FSC® N001967

Printed in Germany

ISBN 978-3-7913-8340-8

www.prestel.com

FILIPPO BRUNELLESCHI
(1377–1446)

LEON BATTISTA ALBERTI
(1404–1472)

DONATO BRAMANTE
(1444–1514)

MICHELANGELO
(1475–1564)

ANDREA PALLADIO
(1508–1580)

GIAN LORENZO BERNINI
(1598–1680)

CHRISTOPHER WREN
(1632–1723)

JOHANN BALTHASAR NEUMANN
(1687–1753)

1300   1400   1500   1600

TIMELINE